MEN
will be
BOYS

M E N
will be
BOYS

the modern woman explains football and other amusing male rituals

sally jenkins

DOUBLEDAY New York London Toronto Sydney Auckland

PUBLISHED BY DOUBLEDAY
a division of Bantam Doubleday Dell
Publishing Group, Inc.
1540 Broadway, New York, New York 10036

DOUBLEDAY and the portrayal of an anchor with a
dolphin are trademarks of Doubleday, a division of
Bantam Doubleday Dell Publishing Group, Inc.

Design by Bonni Leon-Berman

Library of Congress Cataloging-in-Publication Data
Jenkins, Sally.
Men will be boys : the modern woman explains football
and other amusing male rituals / Sally Jenkins. — 1st ed.
    p. cm.
  1. Football. 2. Sex differences (Psychology)
3. Communication—Sex differences. 4. Masculinity
(Psychology) I. Title.
GV951.J47   1996
796.332—dc20   96-19689
                                               CIP

ISBN 0-385-48218-3

October 1996

First Edition

10   9   8   7   6   5   4   3   2   1

acknowledgments

I'M INDEBTED to Esther Newberg of ICM for encouraging me in this lark, and to Bill Thomas of Doubleday for rescuing the manuscript from a state of confusion.

I wish to thank the people who cooperated with interviews, especially the gentlemen of the NFL and college football who understood the spirit of the thing.

Above all a salute with deep affection to the long list of babes who contributed in one way or another, whether with laughs, sheer attitude, or bad title ideas: Nicole, Mary, the Nancys, the Robins, Johnette, Rachel G., Julie C., and all of the Lake Powell habitues.

I was tempted to dedicate this book to Frank Sinatra Jr., with whom I feel I have something in common, but I think I'd rather address it directly to my father, who Frankensteined me, and my mother, who knew exactly what was going on all those years ago when she heard thumps from the back of the house. "Sally," she would call, her voice drifting down the hallway, "leave your brothers alone."

contents

part three
MEN *will be* BOYS

part one

EXES *and* OHS

the modern *woman*

WE GET it, okay?

It doesn't take a genetic imprint. We get the Beauty and the Nuance. We get the Violence and the Ballet. We get the concept of War Without Death and the Lure of the Uniform.

It's not the fact that men love football that makes the Modern Woman want to scream, *"Soooouuuueeee,* pig!" at them. It's their assumption that she is incapable of loving it too. This is going to come as an unpleasant shock to the athletic supporter crowd, but the fact is that football, the last bastion of mud-soaked, bleeding male bonding, is increasingly the property of both sexes.

If a guy wants to understand the Modern Woman, the first thing he has to grasp is that she might know as much about football as he does. The next thing a guy has to realize is that the Modern Woman is a Creature of Enormous Complexity. She may love football, but she also likes being the Object of Desperate Desire.

3

Here is the attitude of the Modern Woman: "I am a smoking, burning babe, and don't you dare call me one."

There are lots of us babes out there. Babes who understand a football is not something that got squashed by the car seat. Babes who can give you the over-under. Babes who can talk about flexes and sealing off the back side. Babes who can do Keith Jackson saying, "It's going to be a barn burner today! They're not just going to burn down the barn, they're going to take a couple of corn rows with 'em!"

Babes who realize *Monday Night Football* is not the same game, week after week, on continuous loop, although it might as well be.

Football? A *woman's* game? Surely not. On no other subject have the differences between men and women been more pronounced. Wives have resented it, mothers have feared it, feminists have pointed to it as evidence of the natural male testosterone-fired urge toward oppression (which, of course, it is). In millions of households, game day has been an occasion of passive-aggressive skirmishing—or of outright physical violence, according to much-debated reports of weekend domestic abuse. Conventional wisdom tells us that women, gentled by estrogen, prefer the ballet.

Fine. Except that researchers recently determined that testosterone can be a passive chemical agent, even a friendly one, while estrogen can act as an irritant. Meanwhile a variety of recent surveys cited by the NFL have discovered that a full 40 percent of the league's television audience is female—representing anywhere from 28 to 40 million women.

And they aren't just sitting next to their husbands on the couch. Women are *playing* football. A huge culture is thriving at universities: Thirty or more women's teams annually enter a Sugar Bowl touch football tournament. A national flag football tournament held annually in Key West, Florida, has grown from five teams to thirty-two teams in just five years. At Princeton, where intercollegiate football was born, a crew of well-bred young women won a national championship at rugby in 1995, led by the daughter of Harold Henderson, general counsel for the NFL.

Babes of all description are Doing It: sorority girls, careerists, right-to-lifers, pro-choicers, mothers, motorcyclists, wives, ceramicists (licensed and unlicensed), professors, provocateurs, and Miss Americas. Consider this exchange between Camille Paglia and an interviewer in *Playboy* magazine.

playboy Do you have a favorite TV show?
paglia Monday Night Football.

5

What's going on? The Modern Woman, with a toss of her ringlets and a spit shine of her plum brandy fingernail polish, is getting in the game, that's what. Over the last twenty-five years, there has been an enormous shift in how women participate in and view sporting events. In 1971, two years before Billie Jean King defeated Bobby Riggs at the Houston Astrodome, only 294,000 girls played varsity high school sports: one in every twenty-seven. Today, one in every three wears a letter jacket, more than two million. And they include roughly 350 women who are active members of high school football teams, playing side by side with men.

Women outspent men in 1994 on athletic gear and sports paraphernalia. They are the fastest-growing segment of golfers. Their marathon times are creeping closer and closer to those of men. And they list football as their favorite sport to watch, according to NFL marketing research.

It seems that we are in danger of becoming what we have been complaining about for centuries: football-crazed, snack-snorting louts.

The conclusion here is obvious.

Women are pigs too.

But we are female pigs. That much is also clear as we surge toward the playing field in ever-greater numbers. Football from the female perspective is a radically different proposition. In the opinion of Joe Gibbs, the NBC color analyst who was a three-time Super Bowl–winning coach with the Washington Redskins, "Women appreciate the game, but they *see* it differently."

His opinion is seconded by Dr. Lawrence Wenner, director of the University of San Francisco's Sports and Fitness Management Program and editor of *The Journal of Sport and Social Issues.* "The fact that female viewers are there doesn't mean they are having the same experience," he says.

Emphatically not. The female sports explosion has not served to close gender divisions—as was so fervently hoped by feminists of the 1970s—as much as it is highlighting once more that there are profound differences between men and women (the chief one being that our side generally smiles more). Indeed, there are Grave Philosophical Debates still to be resolved.

Like, how come the only homework fathers ever help with is the math?

Why is it always the mother who has to cut out all nine cardboard rings for the third-grade Saturn project?

Is it true that a woman's greatest fear is being attacked and a man's greatest fear is being laughed at?

The Modern Woman's best friend, Missy, once tried an experiment. Missy, who is a Modern Woman too, theorized that you could cure males of the urge to bear arms if you never exposed them to guns. She used her infant son, Max, as a test case.

No toy lasers. No cowboy six-shooters. For years she palmed geeky stuff off on him.

Abacuses. Planetariums. Place mats that charted evolution.

When he was seven, he chewed his toast into the shape of a gun, pointed it at his baby sister, and said, "Bang. You're dead."

If women are having an alternative football experience, exactly what kind is it? Do we like football for the same reasons as men or different ones? Can it possibly mean to us what it means to them, having served for centuries as a sacred male ritual and an excuse for female exclusion? Of course not. Football is about how men behave in large groups (not good). It is about boys being with boys, doing the things that boys do.

The following conversation takes place between men and women across America every autumn weekend:

"You hate football," he says accusingly.

"I don't hate football," she says. "I just don't like your friends."

In fact, football, for all that it is becoming a shared common experience, is one of the last great battlegrounds in the war of the sexes. If women find football a compelling game, we also find it essentially hostile, an ubermale exercise in which female roles have historically been restricted to purely decorative ones: dates, cooks, or pom-pom girls.

To Dinosaur Guys, increasingly threatened by the Scary New Women and politically correct nazis of the modern world, the game is a fortress of masculinity, representing traditional sexual relations in an age when the acceptable range of behavioral choices for women seems to be widening alarmingly. Women are encroaching everywhere—in the military, on Wall Street. And now on the playing field and in the stadiums too?

"Men are clinging to football on a level we aren't even aware of," says *Washington Post* columnist Tony Kornheiser. "For centuries, we ruled everything, and now, in the last ten minutes, there are all these incursions by women. It's our Alamo. It's the last holdout. If it goes, I've got to grab the last helicopter out of Saigon."

So is there perhaps a little note of revenge in our growing interest?

Dr. Margaret Carlisle Duncan, a professor of human kinetics at the University of Wisconsin–Milwaukee, has studied the behavior of the sexes as football spectators and concluded that women, while knowledgeable and engaged fans, are also quietly resentful ones. "Women get pleasure and empowerment from subverting and making fun of football," she says. "In part because it's clear to them that it's an all-male institution that celebrates exclusively male values, such as brutality and aggression."

The Modern Woman believes men have kept football from us for too long, because they knew what might happen if they let us in on it. As babes invade playing fields and sports bars, we are growing more self-assured by the minute, developing our own distinct methods, philosophies, and opinions about sport, some of which are deeply threatening to guys.

Take Missy's other child, Molly, the three-year-old. Not long ago Missy's husband, Bill the Thrill, asked Molly what she wants to be when she grows up.

"Me," Molly said.

So maybe it's high time *we* explained football to *them.* Along with a few other things, such as who the Modern Woman is and what she really wants. If she displays a few contradictions, well, what do you expect? She's a pig too. She has her *own* double standards.

First of all, the Modern Woman is not impressed.

The Modern Woman is active, not decorative.

The Modern Woman has never once referred to halftime as "intermission."

The Modern Woman can, when she chooses, employ the hearty language of a stevedore.

The Modern Woman believes that being female is sort of like being left-handed and that she could show a pretty good southpaw delivery if the rest of the world would stop treating it like a handicap.

The Modern Woman has weighed the home versus career dilemma and decided to view it like religion and science: She's never going to reconcile the two, but one is pretty lame without the other.

What really ticks the Modern Woman off is the twisted logic of guys in government who want to dabble in welfare, housing, and child-care issues but who surely won't be showing up on Big Brother Day to help with the kids. You want to help her? Stay out of her way.

The only thing that confuses the Modern Woman about the men who play football is how much money they make.

Is there anything in football that women, by nature, cannot grasp? On the contrary. From our fresher, left-handed perspective, we may understand football better and see it more clearly than men, who, immersed in football's myths and traditions since childhood, have lost all perspective

on the subject. Football, as practiced by the NFL
and the NCAA, is a great game but a lousy sport.

Thus far, there has been nothing for women
in the football culture—nothing acknowledging
them or welcoming them. This, then, is for football babes everywhere, from cheerleader to center. It is meant to enlighten and illuminate. To
give historical perspective and locker-room reality. To make fun of men. To make fun of women.
To swap highbrow spit with common sense. To
state the obscure and to state the obvious.

Let's face it. The Modern Woman likes an emotionally gripping confrontation that results in a
mass catharsis just as much as the next guy.

She's just a little more circumspect about it,
that's all.

Take this book. It supposed to be a women's
guide to football. When, really, we all know it's
a men's guide to how to stop being such pigs
about it.

the *feminine* side

THERE IS something we have been wondering about. It has been bothering us for some time now, so we are just going to come straight out with it. Why do coaches wear those beltless pants?

And another thing. Why is the fullback called a *full*back when he is only *half*way back, while the halfback is called a *half*back when he is *all* the way back?

These are the things that prey on our minds, that nag at us and keep us up at night. Women grasp most of the finer points of the game. We watch and we study—and we root. And yet, even to those of us with a lifetime of experience watching and playing, the game often seems to fly in the face of common sense.

Both scientific and anecdotal evidence suggest that women quite literally perceive the football field differently than men do. Take the halfback-fullback issue. Women see it in terms of distance.

13

Men see it in terms of size. We pay attention to disparate things. We have a different set of concerns. And we have a different set of values.

"Men want to know the score," says NBC Sports president Dick Ebersol, "and women want to know the whole story."

Guys concentrate on specific plays and strategies that result in a final score that will leave them either exuberant or foul-tempered for the remainder of the day. Women see a whole range of behavior, much of which, frankly, looks dumb to us. So if guys think we ask stupid questions, well, sometimes it's a stupid subject.

Two men sat in a restaurant, exhaustively discussing a big upcoming game. Next to them their wives listened, faintly bored.

"Who do you think will win?" one of the men asked.

"What are their animals?" his wife replied.

It's questions like this that give guys facial tics. But to us, it's a reasonable—and typically sardonic—line of inquiry. What she meant was: "You know how you guys are always attaching idiotic mascots to the sports teams you talk about so incessantly? Well, I was just curious. What are these particular yahoos called? The Orange Bloodhounds?"

14

In general, most men watch football from the inside out. First, they focus on the action in the trenches, to see if the offensive line surges forward to run-block or backward to pass-block. Next, they focus on a certain position or matchup. Lastly, they follow the ball.

"I hate going to a game with him," says Jan Wannstedt, wife of Chicago Bears coach Dave Wannstedt. "He follows a specific thing, a position. To me, he misses the whole play."

This is what football looks like to the female spectator: large men forming piles.

We see large men forming piles in a huge stadium, while fans in polyester and primary colors scream at a swatch of green field. As the piles of large men claw at each other, smaller gnatlike figures run circles around them. Meanwhile guys in tacky windbreakers, wearing headphones, yell and fiddle with their dials on the sidelines. Where guys see a marvelous, organized flow, we see piles of men.

"In all of my years watching football," says Joan Tisch, wife of New York Giants co-owner Bob Tisch, "I can honestly say that I have never once confused football with the ballet."

Commentator Larry Merchant theorized in his collection of essays *And Every Day You Take Another Bite* that guys view the game more superficially. "Men attend, women comprehend," he wrote. Merchant tells of going to an Eagles–Steelers game with a date on a sun-dappled Sep-

15

tember afternoon. The field was a plush green, with yellow- and white-chalked sideline stripes.

she They look like dandelions.
he No, love, the Eagles and the Steelers.
she Dandelions. Look. They look like dandelions, running around, blowing in the wind.

Merchant gazed at the field. He saw the yellow and white chalk of the yard lines, the Eagles streaking to and fro in green jerseys with green helmets, the Steelers in yellow jerseys with yellow helmets. And he had to admit that she had a point.

It happens over and over. When Leon Lett sacks Rodney Peete, Harry roars with approval. Next to him, his wife, Doris, says, "Why are they called the Lions when there aren't any lions in Detroit?" Harry stares at her, dumbfounded. "What are you talking about?" he says, assuming she just doesn't get it, when in fact quite the opposite is true. Doris gets it. She just gets it in her peculiarly female commonsensical way.

Joan Tisch and her fellow spousal co-owner, Ann Mara, badger their husbands incessantly to replace the AstroTurf in Giants Stadium with real grass. (They have yet to receive a satisfactory answer as to why this is so difficult.)

Cheryl Smith, wife of Missouri coach Larry

Smith, teaches football to women in a series of annual clinics. Once, shortly after Cheryl delivered a lecture on the importance of the quarterback-center exchange, using volunteers to demonstrate the procedure, a woman stood up with a concerned expression.

"I've been worried about something," she said. "The center. He's got the quarterback's hand in his crotch and then the nose guard is going to *hit* him?"

Cheryl, fifty-five, has been teaching football to women for more than fifteen years. She started giving the clinics when her husband was an assistant coach at Tulane in 1979 as a way of being more involved with his career. The evolution of her interest in the game charts that of many women.

First, as an undergraduate at Ohio State, Cheryl went to games as social outings. "I could have cared less," she says. But when she married Larry, she began to educate herself about the sport that so consumed her husband. "It was a survival tactic," she says. Then she became a rabid fan in her own right. Cheryl has noticed the same progression in the women who have attended her classes, which have numbered as many as 300 at a time, over the years.

This is the female progression: from self-defense to self-satisfaction.

A head coach is home for just a few hours a week during the season. Many wives combat the separation by becoming more involved with their husbands' world. "Why go through your life a miserable bitch?" says former Miami coach Howard Schnellenberger's wife, Beverlee. A onetime majorette for the CFL Montreal Alouettes, Beverlee met Howard in Montreal when he was a player. "It's not a game," she says, "it's a lifestyle." Recently, Beverlee put up a goalpost in the backyard of their home. She likes to hold kicking contests at their cocktail parties and barbecues.

Jan Wannstedt grew up playing touch football with two brothers in the Pittsburgh area, where she met Dave in high school. She and Dave started dating when they were fifteen. Like Cheryl, Jan gives football clinics for women. She first had the idea twenty years ago at Pitt. "Because I felt sorry for all the women in the stands around me who spent more time socializing and worrying about what they were wearing," Jan says. When Dave was an assistant with the Dallas Cowboys, Jan turned her idea into reality. She launched a hugely successful series of clinics with the backing of Cowboys owner Jerry Jones. At her first one, Jan had 125 students. Within two years, the class had grown to 600 women.

Cheryl's classes are sometimes more akin to performance art. She uses a variety of ruses and metaphors to explain the finer points of football strategy, including physical mimicry to show what is going on inside those large pileups. She pantomimes a Heisman Trophy pose. She does a belly dance to demonstrate a linebacker "flowing" to the ball. She mimics a striptease while she explains how men climb in and out of their more elaborate pieces of equipment.

Cheryl finds that women are interested in the more human aspects of the game, not the cold strategy. Men watch football the way they watch video games, following little bionic figures that race across the screen. Women, on the other hand, want to know: What exactly does the head coach do with those headphones? And how much time does he spend with his kids? How do players dress for games?

"Basically, women want to know the personal details," Cheryl says.

Cheryl and Jan agree on three things: 1) that whereas women ten years ago were either enrolled by their husbands or signed up to please their husbands, now they are signing up for themselves; 2) that women's knowledge of the game has grown exponentially; and 3) that many of the women who raise their hands to ask a question begin by saying, "My husband wants me to ask you this . . ."

The fact is, most male fans could learn a thing

or two from their girlfriends. In the estimation of many NFL and college coaches, the average Joe pretends a knowledge that he does not possess. Researcher Larry Wenner has found that men tend to exaggerate their level of knowledge and interest in football because they think they are *supposed* to be avid fans. As Joe Gibbs complains, "Most men think they know more than they do. Here is a sport I've worked all my life at, and my father would call up and want to tell me what plays to run."

The average Jill is a much quicker study, largely because she feels more free to ask questions. Guys wouldn't be caught dead seeming anything less than expert.

Joe Gibbs and Larry Smith concede that there is nothing in football rules or strategy so intellectually challenging that it is beyond the female faculties and can only be fully appreciated by the so-called more studious male turn of mind. Larry, who guest stars at his wife's clinics, says, "I like teaching women better, because they listen. Men take so much for granted. Women ask me things I've never even thought about."

Nobody knows what intelligence really is anyhow. The Modern Woman's best friend, Missy, tells how her seven-year-old, Max, came home one day from school with the announcement that there was a genius in his class. Some egghead kid had graded out as exceptionally gifted. So, of course, her husband, Bill the Thrill, jumped into the discussion.

"Aren't you gifted?" he asked the boy.

"No," Max said glumly.

"Well, maybe if you worked harder, you would be," Bill said.

Missy was about to brain the Thrilling One for giving the kid an inferiority complex, when suddenly Max rallied.

"Hey, Dad," Max said with a hint of truculence. "Were you gifted?"

"I didn't have to be," Bill the Thrill said. "I had other talents."

"Like what?" Max said.

"I had charisma," he said.

If men view football from the inside out, women view it from the outside in, both intellectually and emotionally. Women have developed their affection for the game despite the fact that they have been forced to watch it from the periphery of male enclaves. "It's always been that 'Hey, let's go out with the guys and leave the women at home' thing," says former St. Louis Rams quarterback Chris Miller.

More than just excluded, some women are met with outright impatience or ridicule if they ask their husbands questions. Frequently, the male claim that women "just don't get" football is about protecting their turf. It's the oldest guy ploy in the book: He wants to be left alone in front of the TV. So he tells her she wouldn't understand. "Men make women uncomfortable about it," Jan Wannstedt says, "maybe because they want to keep it a guy thing."

Larry Smith concurs. "I think men exaggerate how complicated football is because it's their domain," he says. "What they're saying is 'This is *ours*.'"

In a 1990 study of male, female, and mixed groups watching football on TV, Dr. Margaret Carlisle Duncan and her human kinetics research partner, Barry Brummett, found that the sexes displayed marked behavioral differences as spectators. In fact, Duncan and Brummett *themselves* displayed radically different viewpoints as they embarked on the study. They argued.

"He said, 'Women aren't real fans. They aren't as involved,'" Duncan says. "And I said, 'That's just not true.'"

Duncan and Brummett recorded the conversations among the three study groups and then analyzed transcripts. In the males-only group, the men showed off their football knowledge to each other, relating background info about the game and the players. In the females-only group, while women displayed sound knowledge of strategy and background, they showed a distinct tendency to make fun of it. They told jokes about the coaches and players. Also, they did not give the game their undivided attention. They did other things simultaneously, such as housework and flipping through magazines.

In the mixed group, the women muted their sarcasm and tended to maintain a distance from the game. One woman went so far as to ask one of the men, "Who are we rooting for?" The women fell into their traditionally peripheral roles and used football talk as a way to try to engage the men.

When Duncan and Brummett analyzed the transcripts, the deflating attitude toward football displayed by the females-only group was striking. "It wasn't that they weren't interested or knowledgeable or appreciative," Duncan says. "It was something else entirely. For various reasons, women like to resist and subvert the game. Although women can get caught up in it, they choose a detachment that allows them to make fun of it."

Which leads us to the ultimate female football question: What is it, women want to know, that obsesses guys to such an absurd extent? What makes a Chicago Bears fan paint his living room like an end zone and refuse to make love to his wife unless she is wearing a team jersey?

What makes the men of Green Bay, Wisconsin,

wear cheeseheads and the men of Cleveland clasp bones in their mouths?

What makes thousands of otherwise sane Georgia gentlemen adorn themselves in red and bark like dogs?

As a rule, women do not do these things. The worst we can be accused of is wearing battery-operated earrings that blink in team colors.

We don't excoriate coaches and spit at them with an out-of-body rage or throw beer cans and chunks of ice at the players on the field. We don't fire a guy like the University of Southern California did Larry Smith, despite the fact that he had taken the Trojans to five bowl games in six years, while doubling the graduation rate of players.

"I don't treat football as life and death," says Cheryl Smith from her executive director's desk at the Regional AIDS Interfaith Network, where she reports to work each morning. "Maybe because I deal with life and death every day."

And yet women can embrace the game in their own ways, which is proven by the wives of players and coaches, some of whom are the most football-literate women in the world—and dedicated fans. "I've been trying to get a headset in the stands for twenty-nine years," Cheryl says.

Unlike many coaches' wives, Pat Gibbs held herself completely apart from football. It was her way of maintaining a semblance of perspective in their lives. Her husband, Joe Gibbs, one of the most renowned workaholics in the NFL, worked so hard that he often slept on a roll-away bed in his office. "My whole life would be passing before my eyes, and she'd say, 'Who're we playing?' " Joe says.

But Pat was paying slightly more attention than Joe thought. After a game, it was Joe's habit to ride home in the car silently, thinking about what had happened on the field that day. He never asked Pat's opinion or discussed his coaching problems. Then one night Joe switched on the car radio and listened to fans criticize his play-calling on a call-in show. Finally he looked over at Pat.

"What do you think?" he asked.

"Well, I do have a question," she said.

"What?" he asked.

"Why do you run up the middle so much?"

"That's the last time I ever ask you anything," he said.

the mouths *of babes*

THE FOLLOWING is a transcript of the first all-female broadcast of a *Monday Night Football* game, which occurred on September 27, 2006, between the Santa Fe Broncos and the Newark Browns. Calling the action were Ros Roberts, the daughter of former Emmy-winning sportscaster Robin Roberts; Brenda Switzer, granddaughter of former Super Bowl coach Barry Switzer; and Imogene Gifford, niece of former ABC analyst Frank Gifford and his TV personality wife, Kathie Lee.

This transcript is the exclusive property of the G.E.–Dreamworks–Gates Group and may not be reprinted, digitalized, or in any other way reprocessed without the express written and downloaded consent of the UniNFL.

ros Hello, everyone, and welcome to the Adobe Dome! It's a lovely evening here—as you can see from the lingering mauve tones of the sunset glistening on the rooftop—and we're pleased to have you with us. Of course, this game doesn't mean a whole lot in the grand scheme of things. It's just football, not childbirth.

imogene Speaking of which, remember, all you youngsters out there, only a small percentage of all college players make it to the UniNFL. Don't let 'em kid you, the average life span in the UniNFL is only a handful of seasons.

ros The Broncos are 10–1 at home in the Adobe Dome—which is hard to imagine, considering the horrendous decor. Wouldn't we love to get our hands on this place for just ten minutes?

imogene Here come the Broncos for their first offensive series, led by quarterback Jeb Burbank, who is really on a tear right now. He leads the league in passing efficiency. Too bad he doesn't lead it in sobriety.

ros Maybe he can live down that DWI arrest by the time the Pro Bowl rolls around.

brenda You know, it wasn't just Burbank's blood alcohol level of 1.3 that was so disturbing to the female sensibility. It was the neighborhood where he was pulled over and the time of day—in the middle of a crowded school district at lunchtime.

imogene Yes, what *about* the children?

brenda Another example of the male entitlement matrix.

imogene Burton, separated, tackles Sperling, two failed marriages. You know, Sperling has

27

really been struggling with injuries. This is his first play from scrimmage in six weeks, since suffering that terrible concussion against Gainesville.

ros We won't show you that replay because it would be in poor taste.

imogene And a source of great pain to his family.

brenda One could argue that the paradigm of violence in the UniNFL is the ultimate expression of male rational argumentation—indeed, of misogyny. A better model might be the cooperative feminine construction.

imogene There goes Rob Carter, the father of three children by three different women when he was at Florida State, sliding off-tackle for six yards.

ros It's a shame that Carter's such a deadbeat dad, because he cuts a wonderful figure on the field.

imogene (*writing on the Telestrator*) I agree. He's got two girls and a boy—their names are Karen, Dierdre, and Kevin—and we'd like to say hello to them and to all their moms out there. This is Carter's new unlisted phone number, in case you've been having trouble reaching him again. For you fans who may not know this, Carter has a habit of dropping out of sight between seasons.

28

ros Oh, my. Look at that Bronco rooting section over there. Those horse masks are really unsightly.

brenda I find a disconcerting correlation between men and severed animal heads.

imogene Play-action, there goes Mel Barr, the notorious womanizer, downfield on the post! Burbank's got him! Burbank to Barr, forty-five yards on the reception to the Newark two!

ros (*drawing on the Telestrator*) The way this play works is, Burbank makes an artistic little fake to the halfback, Carter. See, he just dabs the ball at him. Carter then sashays through the line, tying up the linebackers, while Barr puts a move on the defensive back that looks just like a hula.

imogene They say Barr really gets around.

ros The joke among the Broncos is: When you ask Barr what he's been doing, he says, "The phone book."

brenda Totally inappropriate behavior.

ros And that's the end of the half. I thought the Broncos put together a really beautiful bouquet of plays on that last drive . . .

(*The Microball Halftime Report.* Segment 1: Weekend highlights. Segment 2: An interview with the *Monday Night Football* Mother of the Week, Maude Shula, mother of Brick Shula, the first third-generation UniNFL coach.)

imogene And we're back for the opening kickoff of the second half. Dan Dierdorf asked me to pop his favorite restaurant on-air, but I'm not going to do it because that always drove me crazy when I used to watch this show. Instead, I'd like to warn all you moms out there about the dangers of olestra. Okay, here we go. Slerman fields the kickoff on his own twenty. He crosses the thirty . . . and he's knocked out of bounds at the thirty-two.

ros I hate it when they do that.

imogene What?

ros He's about to step out of bounds and the other guy hits him anyway.

imogene Me too.

brenda Men in groups.

ros You said it.

imogene Uh-oh. The center, Langway, is being helped to the sidelines. It looks like a knee sprain. That's got to hurt. Here it is on the replay.

ros I can't watch.

imogene Langway is one of our favorite men up here in the booth. In the off-season, he writes children's books.

brenda He's very sensitive, with a very strong feminine side, and he's not afraid to show it.

ros Here comes Langway's replacement, Butts. Boy, does he look like he's been hitting the hoagies or what? I don't know about you, but for me, these overweight linemen really ruin the aesthetic.

30

brenda The primal male taste for processed cold cuts never ceases to amaze. Don't these guys ever think of their long-term health?

ros As if.

imogene That Butts, he's big as a house, huh, Ros?

ros What exactly do you mean by that?

imogene Just that he's big.

ros Are you insinuating I should know?

imogene First and ten for the Browns. Steinway, single, takes the snap, hands off to Schmidt, twice-divorced, for a gain of three.

ros The new Broncos uniforms are a big improvement over the old ones. The silver piping has a nice muffling effect on that deep blue. I have never understood the UniNFL's obsession with primary colors.

imogene Schmidt for four. But there's a handkerchief on the play. Say. Why *do* they call it a flag?

brenda Because it's a symbol of the jingoistic male military-industrial obsession. If you examine the tools used on the field, you'll find they are each emblematic.

ros Those tacky yardage markers?

brenda Phallic staffs.

imogene First and fifteen for the Browns. Steinway rolls left, he looks back across the field, and he finds Bledsome, the confirmed wife batterer, for a nineteen-yard pickup and a first down!

ros Patty, if you're out there listening, just take the kids and go.

imogene Steve Bledsome might seem like a real charmer, folks, but when he gets home there's nothing charming about him.

brenda *(writing on the Telestrator)* Patty, our hearts are with you. If you ever need someone to talk to, here's my number.

ros He won't change unless he has to, Patty.

imogene The Browns have called a timeout and there goes Steinway to the sidelines to discuss the situation with his head coach, Brick Shula. I think Steinway wants to go for the touchdown here, but he's going to lose the argument. We can see him nodding his head and saying, "Yes, sir."

ros There is something unseemly about a grown man saying, "Yes, sir," unless he's in the Army.

brenda I couldn't agree more.

imogene Here comes the kicker, Bard, for the field goal attempt.

ros Oh, ick, he's crossing himself.

imogene Like God really takes an interest.

brenda You know, Imogene, I think there's a real chill on the Newark sideline.

imogene What makes you say that?

brenda It's just a feeling I get. They don't look at each other. They don't talk to each other. I think they really need to work on their communication skills. A little channeling never hurt anybody.

imogene There's the two-minute warning. Broncos, first and ten at their own twenty-five. It looks like Burbank is suffering from some pain in his throwing elbow. Brenda, you've got a medical background, don't you?

brenda Actually, I'm a midwife.

imogene What's your view of the injury situation in the UniNFL?

brenda I think the league needs to take a good hard look at alternative medicine: Chinese herbs, acupuncture, Native American medicine cards. I would prefer to see a much more holistic approach to treatment. I really have a problem with this macho attachment to needles.

imogene Burbank to Transom, twelve yards. That's a big first down, because the Broncos can just run out the clock. What a costly decision by Coach Shula there late in the fourth, don't you think, Brenda?

brenda Probably. But, you know, when you look at the bigger picture, what's the relevance?

imogene How about you, Ros?

ros I'd bring in a good landscaper and some ceramic tile and put a really bold green in the upper deck. And I'd completely redo the food at the concession stands.

the ladies' draft

WOMEN WHO think football has nothing to offer them should think again. Where do they think guys got their ideas of innate superiority? And wouldn't they like a piece of *that* action?

Football can provide us with valuable lessons in naked self-serving aggression.

Take a group of men. Put them in a vacant lot, hand them a football, and tell them to choose up sides. First, they pick captains. The captains automatically pick the best players. If they don't, they know they'll never get to be captain again.

Now take a group of women, put them on the same lot, and tell them to choose up sides.

This is what we do.

1) For our first pick, we take our Best Friend.

2) With our second pick, we choose the Most Popular Girl.

3) Third, we pick the woman we want for our New Best Friend.

4) For our fourth pick, we choose the Worst Player, because we feel sorry for her.

5) And with our fifth pick, we do the one thing a guy would never do.

We give it away.

We turn to our Best Friend and we say, "Who do *you* want to pick?"

Those guilty stereotypes we harbor about men and women? They're true. While it's not fashionable among women to admit to anything other than total gender equivalency, the fact is that clearly marked sex differences exist. When scientific data intersects with common sense, major gender divides are hard to deny.

Let's face it.

Men invented: noogies, Indian burns, zorbits.

Women invented: rocking, cooing, cradling.

Men invented: hot dogs, burgers.

Women invented: crudités, condiments.

Men invented: hazing, paddling, horsewhipping.

Women invented: whispering campaigns.

And men invented football, a cross between high-velocity chess and assault with a deadly weapon. Any discussion of men and women and football must begin by conceding the game's utter, essential maleness.

The male taste for games of military strategy and physical conflict is not just a cliché. Social psychologists are willing, with caution, to state that men appear to be more aggressive and better at spatial tasks, such as chess and physics, while women seem to have greater empathy and better verbal skills. In addition, men seem to be more assertive and direct, women more cooperative. (Researchers have also observed that even the male worker bee has a tendency to sexually harass.)

According to Alice Eagly, a professor of psychology at Northwestern University who specializes in meta-analytical research into behavioral sex differences, "In general, these sex differences in social behavior appear consistent with the widespread belief in our culture that women are more socially skilled, emotionally sensitive, and expressive than men, as well as more concerned with personal relationships."

Eagly maintains that aggression is one of the most clear-cut sex differences: In general, men are markedly more aggressive. Particularly when it comes to inflicting physical harm or pain.

Some patently physical differences must also be acknowledged. This much we know:

Women bear children.

The average adult guy is five inches taller than the average female.

Males average 40 percent muscle and 15 percent body fat, while females average 23 percent muscle and 25 percent body fat.

To sum up:

Men and women act different. Also, they look different.

• • •

When the Modern Woman related this to her best friend, Missy, she received a snort in reply.

"No duh," Missy said.

Missy then reported that her seven-year-old, Max, came home one day with a homework assignment from his third-grade teacher, Mrs. Hancock, to name all the animals that provide good things for humans.

He started out fine. "Chickens give us eggs," he wrote. "Cows give us milk."

Then he ran dry. So he asked his father, Bill the Thrill, for some help.

"Alligators for handbags," Bill the Thrill said. "Whales for whale oil."

"Bill!" Missy said.

"Elephants for their ivory tusks," he said. "Minks for their fur . . ."

Missy sighed. "It was a poacher's paradise," she said. "A predator's parade."

The question is not whether differences between the sexes exist, but why? Which of them are inherent and which are social constructions? Do men possess a "war gene"? Do women have an "insecurity gene"? Are females just naturally nicer people?

These are highly politicized topics. Some researchers contend that such a line of inquiry is counterproductive and even dangerous, because it can feed sexism. To admit differences might be to admit inferiority and give ammo to chauvinists. Others maintain gender differences are hard to state categorically and are therefore inconsequential.

The problem is that the generalizations of egghead social scientists are frequently contradicted by the individual peculiarities of actual humans. For instance, a strong case can be made that the differences *within* the sexes are as great as the differences *between* them, whether biological or behavioral.

Some men are ten inches shorter than others. And some women like guns.

Interestingly enough, Eagly finds that the aggression gap between men and women is smaller "for aggression that produces psychological or social harm," as opposed to physical harm. Meaning, women have their aggressive tendencies too but tend to keep them under wraps.

One study of children between the ages of six and fourteen at play shows that boys issue commands and gravitate toward games that involve direct conflict—like football—while girls tend to *propose* rather than command. The same study found that girls play games that are more circumspect, such as skipping rope or "foursquare," which involves bouncing a ball to one another. On closer examination, however, there is a subtle form of competition taking place between the girls. They are trying to get other girls "out" so they can get their best friends "in" the game.

There is a layman's term for such behavior. It's commonly known as backbiting.

The layman is tempted to go even further and declare that, while men are more confrontational, women are surreptitious, and while men are physically stronger, women are incorrigibly sardonic.

"Female aggression is alive and well," actress Ali MacGraw told an NFL Films team researching the responses of women to football. "It's very treacherous, and very subtle, and very veiled, and very mean, and very deadly. But we don't throw the full weight of our bodies at someone else and then hope they don't get up."

Stealth pigs.

Researchers would have migraines trying to figure out nature-nurture issues when it comes to the children of NFL players and coaches. Former New York Giants quarterback Phil Simms's children follow predictable gender patterns. His seven-year-old son has shown an immediate grasp of football, while his eleven-year-old daughter could care less. Also, his son is better in math. "My son is already versed in the concepts of football, and my daughter has no clue," he says. "But I know I treat her different. I just know I do."

Arizona Cardinals quarterback Boomer Esiason's three-year-old daughter, Sydney, has been a genetically loaded terror from the moment she entered the world.

"Her nickname is Sid Vicious," Esiason says. "She's a tornado. She'll probably want to play football. And I'll let her."

Chicago Bears coach Dave Wannstedt has two daughters, Keri, eighteen, and Jami, fourteen, who have been throwing footballs in the backyard since they were toddlers. The only thing Dave insisted on was that they learn to launch a proper spiral. "Don't throw like a girl," he said. In 1995, Keri was ejected from a high school flag football game for unnecessary roughness.

Joe Gibbs can personally testify to the broad spectrum of behavior within the sexes. He has a perfect example within his household in the form of his two football-playing sons, Koy and J.D. They have profoundly different constitutions. Koy feels every small ache, but J.D. has been known to break bones without a murmur.

"One kid shakes like a leaf," Joe says. "But the other, if he says his stomach kind of hurts, you better take him to the hospital, because something's seriously wrong."

Joe doesn't have much use for concepts like socialization. He comes down firmly on the side of genetic loading. When J.D. was in the fourth grade, his teacher requested a meeting with Joe.

She was concerned that J.D. was too preoccupied with physical matters. Every essay he turned in had to do with something active, whether it was football or riding his bike. Perhaps, the teacher advised Joe, J.D. could do with a little food for the soul, some exposure to art or music.

"I was thinking, 'Have I warped this kid?' " Joe says. "Football has been my whole life."

So Joe went home and had a talk with J.D. Maybe he needed some music and art, Joe suggested. Maybe they had put too much emphasis on sports, instead of the life of the mind.

"You gotta be kidding me," J.D. said.

"Yeah," Joe said. "You're right."

Conversations like that drive Pat Gibbs crazy. She accuses her husband and sons of being ubermale elitists.

"That's just great," Pat said at the dinner table one night. "So everyone's worth is purely physical."

"That's right," Joe said. "Kill 'em if they can't block."

Football, of course, is largely responsible for many of the behavioral sex differences in boys and girls. In fact, it probably runs second, behind androgens and just ahead of Barbie, as a factor in shaping gender-patterned behavior. Play, after all, is the chief method by which young mammals learn their survival skills.

41

The following statistics should be required reading for all of the small girls in the United States who are currently playing with Barbie and watching Disney films but who will someday have to earn their own livings.

Eighty percent of women executives at Fortune 500 companies described themselves as having been tomboys in their childhood, according to a study by the University of Virginia's Dr. Linda Bunker.

Girls who play sports are 80 percent less likely to be involved in unwanted pregnancy, 92 percent less likely to be involved with drugs, and three times more likely to graduate from high school, according to the Institute for Athletics and Education.

Obviously, many supposedly inherent female predispositions are not so much a matter of chromosomes as of chronic patronizing. Competitively, women are starting five yards deep in our own end zone. The problem is lack of practice. Babes have been historically benched, while men have been barging around indulging their baser hormonal instincts unchecked though the centuries. Of course we are less aggressive. Wouldn't you be if you had been forced to suppress your every chemical surge, indentured by White Male Oppressors to serve in purely decorative capacities?

Consider the social constraints that babes had to deal with in the eighteenth and nineteenth centuries. Between 1725 and 1845, more than half of an American girl's education—if she received any education at all—focused on needlework. Numerous young ladies from affluent families attended specialty schools famous for the craft.

The Modern Woman would not have survived it. She could never pass for an ornament.

There is only one instance when the Modern Woman doesn't mind being ornamental. When it comes to sweeping under the couch, she would much prefer to lie on it.

The clearest evidence of this is the startling alteration in women's athletic behavior in the last twenty-five years. Historically, we have made a grave misjudgment: We have taken the female antipathy to physical harm to mean a natural lack of competitiveness. In fact, they are not at all the same things. It is a crucial distinction. Ever since the passing of antidiscriminatory legislation in 1972 that allowed girls to play sports freely with boys, including tackle football, women have gradually broadened their range of competitive behavior.

Boomer Esiason and his wife, Cheryl, fell in love when they discovered they shared a child-

43

hood hero in Baltimore Colts quarterback Bert Jones. Former New York Giants running back Herschel Walker's wife Cindy knew nothing about football when they married twelve years ago, but now she asks him why the receiver didn't get more separation from the defensive back. "Men haven't changed, women have," says Walker. "I think women are becoming more aggressive in everything they do."

Progress, however, is halting. That's because of Barbie. Instead of being encouraged to play forthright competitive games, girls continue to be presented with the lithe figure and depressing décolletage of Holiday Barbie, Ballerina Barbie, *Princess* Barbie.

This is the Mattel toy company's idea of social advancement:

There used to be one Barbie with forty-seven outfits. They were called things like Solo in the Spotlight and came with tiny stiletto heels that played hell with the vacuum cleaner.

Now there are forty-seven Barbies.

Waikiki Barbie. Baywatch Barbie. Civil War Nurse Barbie. The toy chest in a little girl's bedroom looks like a concentration camp: a tangle of naked emaciated limbs.

It's time Barbie got with the program.

I want Prime Minister Barbie.

Kickboxer Barbie.

Appellate Court Judge Barbie.
Frieda Kahlo Barbie.
Flight Commander Barbie.

There is one existing Barbie that the Modern Woman approves of. She dominates the window at F. A. O. Schwartz in all her splendor every Christmas. Her name is Goddess of the Sun Barbie and she costs $300. The Modern Woman likes her because she looks imperious.

What we need is any kind of Barbie who would suggest to small girls that estrogen is not nearly the gentle little hormone it has been portrayed as. Actually, as any mother can attest, it leads to a sharp rise in insolent behavior among young women.

The day is not far off when girls will be allowed to learn the pleasure of physically moving another human being out of the way, just as boys do. In women like Cheryl Esiason, we are seeing the coming of age of the first generation of girls who are growing up playing and watching football alongside their dates. Pittsburgh Steelers running back Jerome Bettis theorizes that the gender differences around football will be significantly smaller when women have the same lifetime of practice at roughhousing that men do. "Maybe guys can relate to the physical nature of it a little

45

bit better, but that's just because they get hit from a young age," Bettis says. "Each person has their own reasons for being out there, but the common ground is that they're competitive. Women can relate, you know, even if it's, like, get that flag."

Could women ever be comfortable hitting each other? Perhaps. Just look at how comfortable we are hurting each other's *feelings*.

Social scientists agree: With practice, women might become as inured to physical contact as men. But that raises another awkward political question: Why, now that we are learning the game in significant numbers, are many of us sticking to our own particular brand of it, flag football, otherwise known as "powder puff"? A sorehead radical feminist answer might be that we are forced to settle for a marginalized version of the game by Creepy Conspiratorial Men who perpetuate societal role-playing traps.

It's not that complicated. Here's what's really going on: We simply have a problem with a game that requires an ambulance on the field.

As women begin to play sports full-bore, many of us are discovering that we do not *really* want to bridge the Violence Gap between the sexes. Plenty of women are capable of physical contact but take issue with the game's more brutal aspects. And not because of faintheartedness or some fundamental lack of understanding.

We understand the physicality of football all

too well—well enough to know that a good cuffing around is the closest some guys can come to showing public affection for their sons. Daddy wants to be adoring with little Freemont, but he can't flat-out hug him, so instead he bats the toddler around and then hurls him skyward, barely missing the ceiling fan blades that could decapitate him, while Mom and Grandma watch in abject horror.

When Freemont gets a little older, Daddy says, "Come on, hit me as hard as you can." Next, he enrolls him in Pop Warner. And it builds from there, until Freemont is the picture of a swaggering young American male. Or a trembling bundle of neuroses.

"What's the first thing we do when a boy gets in a fight?" Denver Broncos running back Reggie Rivers says. "We congratulate him. I'm not going to say there aren't some women out there who like violence, but it's not like guys. You should see how we get off on a big hit. We can't wait to see it on film, in slo-mo. We cultivate it, and we praise it. We're taught from the time we're kids that hitting people is a good thing."

Joe Gibbs contends that women simply do not realize the extent to which men celebrate the knockout blows they deliver to each other and that it is a natural male trait. "There is a real rush," Joe says. "Men get a thrill, a kick out of it."

Kathy Klope agrees. Klope became the first

woman to play on a NCAA Division I team when she made the Louisville roster as a kicker in 1995. She was taken aback by the behavior of her teammates on the sidelines. "They got real excited by the big hits," Klope says. "They called it 'blowin' 'em up.'"

The Modern Woman's favorite seven-year-old, Max, and his friends act just the same way. One afternoon Max and his best pal, Brent the New Kid—that's what they call him, even though he's lived next door for several years—decided to see what would happen if they dropped their Power Rangers from the tree house. They wanted to watch the little bodies bounce off the ground.

"Wait," Brent said. "Can we light them on fire first?"

For some reason, a taste for conflict has been equated with a taste for harming your fellow man within the male sports community. Women make a major distinction between the two: Physical aggression does not necessarily mean Attack with Intent to Maim.

At least some of the more egregiously violent behavior in the NFL is simply a result of permission and hypermale posturing. Press a guy, and he will admit that football isn't inherently the favorite sport of all men, and that the violence can

48

be daunting for them too. Jerome Bettis's favorite sport as a kid was bowling, but his older brother, Johnnie, insisted that football was more appropriate for a boy. New York Giants receiver Mike Sherrard remembers exaggerated notions of toughness being drummed into him.

"We're told women are supposed to be cheerleaders and men are supposed to be football players—and more than that, we're taught that the violent part is what makes a man a man," Sherrard says.

Then there is Max, who seems to come by his ideas of sexual role-playing naturally. Like the time he got in a water fight with the kids across the street. He seized his baby sister and held her in front of him.

"What are you doing with her?" Missy said.

"Human shield," he said.

"Put her down," Missy said.

"Come on," he said, rolling his eyes. "What else is she good for?"

No wonder some NFL players don't think twice about harming an opponent. New York Jets kicker Nick Lowery went so far as to slap a ballboy in the face on the sidelines one afternoon late in the 1995 season because the ballboy smarted off. In fairness, many guys have no more in common with Lowery than a woman does. The old adage that women can't really relate to football because they haven't been in the trenches is ludicrous in a day and age when, secretly, *most men* can't relate anymore to the savagery that occurs in the NFL.

In fact, many players resent the suggestion by the average male spectator that he shares some kind of natural testicular understanding of the violence. "That guy who says he'd give it all up to play the game for free?" Phil Simms sneers. "I'm, like, 'Yeah, go right ahead.' The fact is, this game is just too hard. You can't do it for nothing."

St. Louis quarterback Chris Miller had reason to question his commitment to the game in 1995 when he received his fifth concussion in the space of fourteen months. The NFL has been searching for a way to curb the gratuitous wounding of quarterbacks that goes on every Sunday. In 1994, a spate of concussions, including blows to San Francisco quarterback Steve Young and to Dallas quarterback Troy Aikman, moved the league to tighten regulations on using the crown of the helmet against defenseless players. It didn't work. Ten different players were fined up to $12,000 for illegally assaulting quarterbacks with their helmets in 1995, and nine quarterbacks suffered severe shoulder injuries.

The most oft-spoken word in the NFL was *"Unnnhhhhh."*

Listening to Chris Miller explain why he continued to play, there was nothing in his words that would seem to elude the female sensibility. Quite the opposite. Miller persisted because of the pleasure he takes in the personal relationships—a supposed hallmark of female behavior. "Honestly, it's not my favorite sport," he said. "Golf is. But the comaraderie is what keeps me playing. There is no better feeling, other than having kids, than celebrating with your teammates after you've taken all those hits and shots. Shit, I've blown my left knee twice, broken my collarbone, and dinged my head a bunch of times. I could be making safer money. But it's the bonds that keep you."

At the end of the 1995 season, however, shortly after he made those remarks in an interview for this book, Miller announced that he would sit out a year on the advice of his doctors, who were concerned by his slow recovery from his last concussion. His symptoms included memory loss and disorientation.

For all of their differences, men and women may understand each other better on the subject of football than they suppose they do. If aggression is a gender divide, bonding is a bridge. There is nothing inherently hormonal in the idea of a shared common goal that can only be reached after a physical ordeal that results in exhaustion.

One reason why men love football is the emotional vulnerability they feel in each other's company when they are mutually fatigued. That is hardly a distinctly male ritual. Ask any group of young mothers.

Phil Simms suspects that men are attracted to the game because it's a rule-breaking experience—they can openly express sentiments and vulnerabilities that they would normally smother in mixed company. "When you do something so well and a hundred of you do it together, the feeling becomes a little spiritual," Simms says. "The barriers aren't there. The cussing, the way you talk to each other, aren't allowed anywhere else. I'm over forty and I've played football all my life and now I have to try to lose some of those habits. I find myself saying things out loud other people can't believe. Then there's the closeness with your teammates, which is breaking another kind of rule. My God, I've patted more men on the ass."

At a 1995 meeting of the Endocrine Society, researchers reported that testosterone by itself did *not* automatically lead to a catalog of Iron John-like behavior. Rather, they concluded, human behavior is contradictory and open to interpretation.

Unless you're a woman, in which case it's all perfectly clear. The Modern Woman has seen plenty of human behavior, and it doesn't look correctable to her. Let's face it. Men invented: belching, pugilism, authoritarian regimes, and war crimes. Women invented: suffering, dieting, vegetable gardens. And laughing and weeping at the same time.

football 101

WOMEN ASK elementary questions about football. So sue us. It's not because we don't comprehend it. We just comprehend it differently. It's a yin and yang, left-brain, right-brain thing.

Our questions make perfect sense when you stop and think about them. Like, how come the big guy in front makes so much less than the smaller guy behind him, who is always so clean?

On any subject, women ask more questions. Also, we ask questions about others. Men ask questions about themselves. That's one of the biggest differences between the sexes. When men ask, "Why me?", women ask, "Why *not* me?"

Also, women are better at answers. We don't stop talking until we have answered a question from every possible angle. Guys only need one word. "Because." It's their favorite reply. It covers everything.

How come it's against NCAA rules to pay college football players, but it's not against the rules to make them wear Nike swooshes so coaches can get six-figure endorsement contracts?

Because.

Ask the question again, and you get the same answer, only this time in two words.

Just because.

More female questions—and some female answers:

Q Why is it called football when they don't use their feet?

A The game is a third-generation mutt, a combination of soccer and rugby, but nobody took the trouble to properly rename it.

Q How come when a guy scores, even his own teammates hit him?

A Because football is sanctioned emotion for men.

Q In sudden death, does someone play dead?

A Sometimes. It's known as choking.

Q How come the NFL fines players for leaving their shirttails out, but if you hit a guy in the back, it's only a penalty?

A Because the game is really governed by the NFL Licensing department.

Q Is there such a thing as the *whole*back, and if not, why not?

A No, because men don't fully commit.

55

Q If a guy is called a *quarter*back, shouldn't there be four of him?

A Not in this game of double standards.

Q Do *tail*backs have tails?

A They certainly act like it when they move in packs, especially in nightclubs.

Q Why is it called a touchdown?

A Originally, in order to score, a player had to touch the ball down on the ground. Then television was invented. Now the end zone looks like the home of the Joffrey Ballet.

Q Does the franchise player work at Burger King?

A Some end up there. Others go to Folsom Prison.

Q If NFL players are so brave, how come none of them have ever come out of the closet?

A Because there are not now, nor have there ever been, any homosexuals in the NFL. Ever. Not one.

Q Why is he called the nose guard when his face is always bleeding?

A *Everybody* is always bleeding.

Q Why is it called a stunt when all they do is move sideways?

A Because it's a sport of overstatements.

Q What is the trainer's chief duty?

A Triage.

Q Is a medial collateral good at the bank?

A Yes. Most of them are heavily insured.

Q How come steroids are against NFL rules, but sexual assaults aren't? Aren't both felonies?

A Maybe because one is harmful to his health, and one is harmful to her health.

Q Why *do* coaches wear those beltless pants?

A Because their weight tends to fluctuate over the course of a season, due to their long hours and terrible eating habits. It is not unusual for them to gain and lose fifteen pounds every fall, so they like pants they can adjust.

Q Will a woman ever play in the NFL?

A Yes. After the big comet collides with earth, the world as we know it will come to an end, and we will begin all over again as primordial slime, only this time we will evolve into a new genderless species with flippers and gills. When that happens, the Modern Woman can say with some assurance, then a babe will play in the NFL.

Q Why are all football players from Texas, Pennsylvania, Florida, and California?

A Why are all *guys* from Texas, Pennsylvania, Florida, and California? Think about it.

   Ever met a guy from Connecticut?

   Other strictly guy states are the Dakotas, Nebraska, Arizona, Minnesota, and the entire Midwest. Colorado and Idaho are bisexual.

Girl states are Oregon, Maine, and Rhode Island. This same principle does not apply to continents, which are of course dominated by world powers, all of which are male. Islands, on the other hand, are almost exclusively feminine: Bali, Tahiti, England.

Q How many football players does it take to screw in a lightbulb?

A None. They've all got someone to do it for them.

Q If AstroTurf causes so many injuries, why don't they just go back to natural grass?

A Because the chiseling owners won't pay to convert the stadiums back.

Q What's a Brown?

A No one knows anymore.

Q Who invented football anyway?

A The same people who invented land rushes and leveraged buyouts.

Q What's so wrong with holding?

A Absolutely nothing. The world would be a better place if we were all held more.

Q Why is it called rushing instead of running?

A To make it sound more important than that.

Q How much money does an owner make?

A Let's open their books and see.

Q Who's number one?

A If he's smart, he'll say, "My wife."

Q Can anyone buy season tickets?

A Sure. Put your name on the waiting list, poison the 10,000 people ahead of you, and they're all yours.

Q Do you have to be smart to play football?

A Only on offense.

part two

DINOSAUR GUYS *and* SCARY *new women*

Leave it to a babe to launch a league with a handful of kitchen ingredients. When the original members of the National Women's Flag Football Association first took the field, they drew their yard lines by hand, crookedly, out of flour and sugar. There were a lot of complaints about the ants.

Finally a local Nellie Bly outlet kicked in a few bucks for a liner and chalk. They were in business. And that's how it all began—with baking goods.

In 1985, an elementary school social studies teacher named Diane Beruldsen recognized that there was a thriving flag football cult among professional women in the New York area and established a league of six teams on a vacant playground in Brooklyn, lining it with her sacks of flour. Ten years later, the league has 2,000 members nationwide. Beruldsen is one of those energetic, missionary types who seethed for years over the fact that there were exactly two sports offered to women when she was an undergraduate at John Jay College: basketball and cheerleading. "Why is it that the most acceptable sports for women are the ones where they wear skirts?" she says.

Teams kept forming, and then growing, and splitting off into more teams. Beruldsen began barnstorming nationally, seeking out female football fanatics to join the league. She painted a mermaid holding a football on the door of her car and started crisscrossing the country, following contacts, chasing rumors. Sometimes she just cruised parks, looking for footballs and long hair flying through the air.

She drove twenty-five thousand miles. In Maryland, she found a team that had been together for fifteen years. There were teams of women cops. Teams of women lawyers. Teams of women accountants. Insurance adjusters, civil servants, and ad execs.

Now thirty-two women's flag football teams from around the nation annually converge on Key West, Florida, every February for a three-day national championship tournament. In 1996, word of mouth had even reached the NFL, which sent a film crew to document the event.

The action sprawls over four fields, overseen by Beruldsen, who does everything from mediate disputes to refill the Gatorade containers, while sporting a variety of caps and T-shirts that say things like FOOTBALL IS LIFE. THE REST IS JUST DETAILS.

Women can't stage an event without turning it into a social occasion with raw vegetables. The concessions sell pita bread sandwiches. But the women who play flag football do not apologize for their feminine rituals. They are not ashamed of their salads, their softball games, and their socials. "We don't want to play like guys," Beruldsen said. "Why should we? We're two different animals."

Beruldsen once played on a flag team with a male coach. He tried to drill the squad in cheap shots. He would stand on the sidelines and scream, "Take 'em out!" Finally the women fired him.

"We said, 'You know, we don't want to break their legs,' " Beruldsen says.

a brief history *of* *time* and *sex*

AT SOME point in the evolutionary process between the act of straightening up and lighting his first fire, man played his first game of football. It is safe to say that at that moment, somewhere nearby a woman rolled her eyes.

In fact, one might view the entire course of Western Civilization this way: men choosing up teams, men conquering other teams, teams of men taking shit that doesn't belong to them.

Football was invented to shore up the male ego in peacetime. The Modern Woman does not have to be a historian or a sociologist to see that. A quick perusal of scholarly texts bears this out. What happened when the frontier closed? Football, that's what.

In fact, the game's most significant periods of growth coincided exactly with crises in masculinity, when social disruptions and feminist movements threatened treasured notions of manliness and Anglo-Saxon superiority. Since time immemorial, men have resolved their anxieties in the simple, primal game of football. "I guess it's how we live out the animal in us," says St. Louis Rams quarterback Chris Miller.

Dr. Michael Messner, a professor at the University of Southern California's Center for the Study of Men and Women, sums up the game's cultural history this way: "It's a brutal and barbaric game that reinforces a value system of violence and aggression, with clear-cut gender divisions between men and women. But that said, I have to admit I like to watch it."

Here's a brief history of the game from the female perspective, which is basically that of someone who has been forced once too often to prepare the halftime meal.

The first recorded signs of football are contained in hieroglyphics suggesting that a game resembling soccer existed in ancient Egypt—and that it was linked to fertility rites. This tradition, of course, continues today. Anthropologists have noted the similarity between Egyptian temptresses and sorority recruiting hostesses.

While men were inventing football, women made those exquisite cave paintings in southern France. Left on their own all day while the men were out, they decided to brighten their drab surroundings in an early precursor to home improvement and invented burnt sienna, ochre, and the first truly modern interiors.

In Greece, a popular sport involved throwing or

67

kicking an object across a goal line. The games were chronicled by guys like Pythagoras, Pindar, and Pericles, who were the first sportswriters.

The Greeks would follow their games with sacrificial banquets and the hacking and hewing of small animals for the purpose of barbecuing, much as we do today. In many an Aegean village, you can still see the ruins of their sports bars.

When Roman legions conquered the Greeks, they spread their version of it around the empire. The Roman jocks were the first great narcissists. They built sculptures and shrines to themselves and called their elite citizens *nobilis,* which back then meant famous, or celebrated. The Romans loved to conquer, and they sent football to such far-flung places as the British Isles and the University of Michigan.

The basic aim of football has changed little over the centuries. It is about bullying the opposition into retreat via a mob action, with only a handful of rules restraining the conduct of those on the field. What few rules do exist are to be circumvented or exploited, or simply changed when things get too boring or nonviolent. "It's about war," says Missouri coach Larry Smith. "I don't know if it's in men's genes or what. But you're out there to hurt the other guy. I mean to absolutely physically destroy him. We promote it, we encourage, hell, we *teach* it."

The first modern ball ever used was the head of a Danish pirate. According to the *Official Encyclopedia of Football,* the ancient Celts kicked around the skulls of Dane invaders. The British Isles were occupied by the Danes from 1016 to 1042, during which time many a pitched battle was fought before the local tribes rose up and drove the Danes back into the sea. Sometime later a farmer digging in his pasture unearthed the skull of a Dane warrior and did an extremely predictable Guy Thing: He booted the skull around the pasture. He was soon joined by other locals, who readily took up the new pastime.

Eventually, someone hit on the idea of inflating the bladders of cows and pigs, as they were easier on the feet than the skulls and bones of dead enemies. Does anyone doubt that this was a *woman's* suggestion?

Futballe, as it was known, swept England. It became a national obsession and took a form more akin to town riots than a game, pitting whole communities against one another. Sometimes called *mellay,* or *mêlée,* the entire populations of two villages—including women, some evidence suggests—would meet at a neutral geographical point. A bladder would be tossed into the street and chaos would ensue. The game would rage through the townships, with crops, fences, livestock, stores, and cottages flattened. The game would end when one team kicked the ball past a goal, which was usually a predetermined boundary like a fence line.

At about this time, the game was adopted by Vasco da Gama, Ponce de León, and other explorers, who applied it to conquering the New World. Trampling everything in their path, they went off in search of the Fountain of Youth, which they believed flowed with a rudimentary form of Gatorade.

This ushered in the first great rivalry in football annals—between Spain and England. Only occasionally would underdogs like France and Italy interfere; they were usually too busy inventing the art history major.

The Spaniards forged ahead in the great rivalry when Christopher Columbus set sail. His ships were called the *Nino,* the *Pinto,* and the *Piña Colada.* Columbus offered a dubloon to whichever of his men could spot America first. He knew he had found it when a dove flew over his prow, carrying an olive branch. It was promptly shot down and roasted on the ship's Smoky Joe Grill.

But the Brits struck back. They won the biggest upset in NCAA history during the Elizabethan Era when they defeated the Spanish Armadas. It was the beginning of the patriotic team concept.

Around this time, a version of the game split off and evolved into something called "association football." Later the name was abbreviated to "assoc.," and still later another version of it was twisted, through slang, to "soccer."

Football became the game of choice at the all-male public schools of England, where it was used to fortify schoolboys' tender ideas of virility. Each English institution developed its own corruptions of the game, depending on the sizes and limitations of their playing fields. At Westminster Abbey, schoolboys played over the stone floors of the great cathedral and called it the Game in Cloister. At Eton, it was called the Wall Game, because it was played along a high brick wall. Teams were limited to eleven players on each side, because the school lacked a large green.

The assumption was—and is—that if boys did not harden themselves and learn to show initiative through football, they would become cringing slaves.

The most significant evolution of football took place at Rugby, where it flourished alongside a concept called Muscular Christianity, a backlash notion against the growing asceticism of religious studies. Muscular Christians held that young aristocrats needed rough games as well as prayer to mold them into strong and virtuous men, capable of wielding the whip of social and political power and holding back the encroaching working-class hordes. The philosophy was popularized in the book *Tom Brown's School Days.* Religion has been inappropriately wedded to football ever since.

In 1823, a Rugby student produced the game's most dramatic variation from soccer with a particularly male display of impatience. William Webb Ellis grew frustrated with a pileup in the middle of the field and picked up the ball and ran with it in an attempt to score before the five o'clock dinner bell. He was disgraced for his breach of sportsmanship, but he went down in history as the first man to run with the ball.

Meanwhile, back in America, the Constitution had been framed, Lewis and Clark had Expedited, and Gold Rushes and Indian Wars were almost over. Harvard, Yale, and Princeton were bored. There was no place left to go if you wanted to be a Rugged Individualist, except to the Donner Party.

Football surged in popularity. Free-for-alls reigned, with entire freshmen and sophomore classes engaging in bitterly fought mob riots. After graduation, many young men went off to Texas to fight Santa Anna and wear coonskin caps and endured much hardship in the name of Manifest Destiny, also known as Take All You Want.

The Modern Woman experienced the effect of Manifest Destiny firsthand the day she taught her favorite seven-year-old, Max, how to play poker.

He refused to bet with matchsticks or nickels.

"Okay, then what do you want to play for?" she asked.

"The beach house," he said.

In 1869, Rutgers challenged the college at Princeton to a game of association football. They met on November 6 in New Brunswick, New Jersey, with twenty-five players to a side and a small black rubber ball that could be kicked or butted with a shoulder. Young men laid aside their hats, coats, and vests and, in shirtsleeves and plain wool trousers, battled themselves bloody and silly and thought themselves marvelous. George Large of Rutgers got knocked clear through a rail fence. Rutgers prevailed, 6–4, in what went down as the first intercollegiate football game.

From then on, schools began to regularly schedule each other. However, there was a problem. There was no lucre or unclaimed territory to be had. Somehow, the winners didn't feel as rapacious as they used to. So they hit on an ingenious solution: Instead of burning villages, they decided to take something of sentimental value from the opposing campus, such as a Revolutionary cannon, a little old oaken brown jug, an axe, a goat, or a ram. Drunken fraternity boys could then spend whole terms plotting to steal them back.

73

Each American school added a wrinkle to the game. Yale's version was influenced by the enrollment of a boy from Eton who brought the Wall Game with its eleven-men squad to New Haven, Connecticut. At Harvard, a Canadian influence was felt in 1874 when a rugby team from McGill University of Montreal visited Cambridge, Massachusetts. The Canadians came bearing a strangely inflated ball in the shape of an oval rather than a perfectly round sphere, so that it was easier to throw. Thus was the Forward Pass invented, soon to be followed by the Tight Spiral.

Hand in hand with these advances spiraled ever more elaborate notions of American elitism, which resulted in things such as the Gold Standard, Episcopalians, and Newport, Rhode Island.

These early American games were so brutal and notoriously bloody, resulting in deaths and catastrophic injuries, that Harvard's Teddy Roosevelt threatened to make the sport illegal. He relented, convinced of football's value in building strong young men who knew how to wield a Big Stick in foreign policy.

It is at this point that women become an integral part of the game's history. Frankly, as far as guys are concerned, from here on we've got no one to blame but ourselves. According to them, if football got out of hand, it's because we *drove* them to it.

Scholars have noted that the emergence of football as a mass spectator sport in the nineteenth and early twentieth centuries went hand in hand with fears that society was becoming "feminized" by industrialization. With the shift from farm labor and small business to corporate capitalism and wage labor, physical abilities became increasingly irrelevant in achieving economic status or political power.

Guys just couldn't get used to saying "textiles" when asked what they did for a living.

Traditional Anglo-Saxon male roles became shakier with other alarming social disruptions: urbanization, the closing of the frontier, the suffragette movement, the swelling immigrant tide, the banning of spittoons, and the supplanting of iceberg lettuce by the more effete romaine.

American men became strikingly preoccupied with their bodies and prowess. Teddy Roosevelt trumpeted "the strenuous life" and mounted stuffed animals all over the White House, while Ivy League scions like Walter Camp and Caspar Whitney espoused football as a game that promoted both manly skills and morals in the ruling classes. Mike Oriard, a former NFL player turned scholar, author, and professor of American literature at Oregon State University, reaches this conclusion in his comprehensive and fascinating cultural history of the game, *Reading Football:* "The outcry against football brutality was great, but concern over the possibility of an emasculated American manhood greater."

Oriard notes that the promotion of football as "manly sport" was accompanied by hyperaggressive foreign policy, the sudden popularity of Western fiction, a bodybuilding craze, and the remaking in the public imagination of the business tycoon into a swashbuckling hero. Basically, American guys in the late nineteenth and early twentieth centuries behaved much as they do in Beverly Hills today. The more diverse and refined cultural habits become, the more testy and imperious guys get.

This may have as much to do with the accompanying deterioration in their cuisine as it does with a backlash against fears of emasculation. Male levels of irritation rise as it gets harder to find a good old-fashioned pan-fried meal over an open fire, made of something that blinks. Consider the proliferation of polenta and alternative-grained breads in California. Also, the invention of hydroponic broccoli. The historical parallel is obvious.

The late-nineteenth century male dread of effeminacy and anxiety over the erosion of his authority were accompanied by a need to preserve traditional ideas of gender differences. And thus was born that open-air coochie-coochie girl, the cheerleader.

Women were crucial to the growing football spectacle—as admirers of manliness. As early as the 1880s, Oriard notes the existence of what TV producers would today call "honey shots" in newspaper accounts of those contests. There had to be women in the stands to certify that these were real men and worthy objects of adoration. Oriard finds story after story in which comely damsel spectators are an integral part of the narrative, reaffirming traditional sexual relations.

The problem is, we didn't do a very good job of it. If we had, then football would never have become what it is today. For Oriard also finds that women were already becoming sardonic critics on the subject of football. He detects "a distinctive feminine irony" in press accounts of early American football.

A disturbing new female type was developing on the American scene: In addition to the cheerleader, the period marked the advent of the self-assured, college-educated, vote-seeking professional woman. She was just one more figure representing social fracture. No one typified the Modern Woman of the late nineteenth century more than Winnifred Black, one of the original so-called "sob sisters." Black was a married mother of three and a dynamic journalist for the William Randolph Hearst newspaper empire whose first assignment was to cover a flower show. She went on to cover the William Jennings Bryan presidential campaign; various famed murder trails, including that of architect Stanford White; the Galveston flood; and the San Francisco earthquake. She was also the first woman to report on a prizefight, covering it from behind a curtained booth. "Men have a world into which women cannot enter," she remarked.

Unless, of course, you take off your clothes, which the Modern Woman does not approve of. The only kind of promiscuity she condones is intellectual promiscuity, and most guys aren't into that.

In 1895, Black was assigned to spend a day with the Yale football team. Employing a tone of hilariously dry condescension, she asks, "Who's Butterworth?", affecting not to know who the team's captain and star was, to the chagrin of her subjects. Black's view of football was that it was a childish exercise played at with hilarious solemnity. Just as it is today.

Mike Oriard's observations about the origins of American football intersect with those of Dr. Michael Messner, who sees two distinct crises of

American masculinity: 1) from the 1890s through the 1920s, and 2) from the post-World War II era to the present. In each case, football's surge in popularity coincided with significant feminist movements. The rise of football as an organized mass spectator sport served as "a primary institutional means for bolstering a challenged and faltering ideology of male superiority in the twentieth century," Messner argues.

With its emphasis on the extreme possibilities of the male body and psyche, coupled with the emphasis on relatively naked, voluptuous women as cheerleaders, football has reinforced traditional notions of male-female relations like no other public ritual. As Messner puts it, football reassures men that "there is at least one place where men are clearly superior to women."

Basically, it's Wishful Thinking in Dudesville.

But something is happening in the 1990s. If, as Oriard and Messner assume, football has been a powerful sexual narrative for the American male from the nineteenth century to the present, then it seems that narrative is in the process of being co-opted by women.

According to various surveys, including Nielsen research, anywhere from 28 to 40 million women watch the NFL on TV each week, and as many as 60 million watch the Super Bowl. League figures show that women make up 40 percent of game day attendance. Forty-six percent of all NFL Licensing purchases are made by women.

What's happening is that women are discovering how deeply satisfying the sanctioned conflict of football can be. Consider the sentiments of Lesley Beverly, a college student who played in the National Women's Flag Football Association tournament in Key West in 1995. "We loved it because we could hit, spit, curse," she said. "It was like we could break all the rules of femininity we grew up with."

As a spectator sport for women, football in the 1990s is far more accessible than it was twenty-five years ago. These days it is less a game of brute strength than one of stratagems, orchestrated by bespectacled coaches speaking techno talk and televised in blazing color. Although violence remains a part of the game, the violence is of a different sort than before, that of elegant individual collisions at ever-higher speeds, as opposed to the bloody mass movements of the past.

There is a comforting clarity in the narrative of a football game that both sexes respond to. It has a beginning, middle, and an end, with a final score. Men and women alike feel anxious in the new age as technology outstrips the human mind and body and as American society becomes ever more sexually confused. The Christian right wants to censor Robert Mapplethorpe, rap music, and grade school textbooks. Multiculturalists want to censor the *Sports Illustrated* swimsuit issue, newspaper columnists, and college textbooks. While women's sneaker sales have shown a marked shift from the decorative to the active, men's moisturizers have also shown a marked rise. It's enough to make you go off into a crop circle and meditate.

Instead, we reassure ourselves by watching football.

chapter seven

a glossary *of* terms

WORDS ARE very low on the list of things men like to say. They speak in codes, terms, euphemisms, diagrams, epigrams, and clichés, but rarely do they make clear, simple statements in comprehensible language. The terminology of football demonstrates that, left to themselves, without women around to force them to elaborate, men would all end up talking to each other via signal lamps and X's and O's.

The needlessly complex dialect of football is a real stumbling block for babes, who fail, very rightly, to understand why so many men insist on referring to the game ball as a "prolate spheroid."

Ask the Modern Woman what a prolate spheroid is, and she'll tell you it's a glandular disease that strikes men over eighteen and makes them talk self-importantly.

Guys use overinflated phraseology when talking football because it makes football sound like an endeavor of the utmost urgency. It's their way

82

of justifying the amount of time they spend at it. They would like to convince us that only a select club of very intelligent men can decipher and absorb all of the sport's intricacies, nuances, and abstractions.

When, really, they're just playing Army. Ever notice how they like to use military phrases? Phrases like: bombs, trenches, blitzes, drafts. And sexual ones: going deep, penetrating.

Example: A coach is giving his halftime chalk talk. Here's what he says: "We have to reassess our schemes. We've got to seal off the back side and get some penetration. Offensively, we aren't picking up the blitz, we're making all the wrong reads, and we aren't doing anything in the red zone."

Translation: What he means is "We better do some fast thinking. We've got to stop that little son of a bitch from running all over us. The other team is making us look like our pants are down around our ankles, and the one time we had a chance to score we just fucking sat there."

What if the head coach was a woman? Here's what she might say: "I really feel that we need to discuss a few things. I'm not seeing a sense of togetherness on defense, and I'm getting from a few of you that you feel threatened. I want you to know that I sympathize, but you've got to push through it and get to the other side of your emotions. And I really think that on offense we need to be more giving."

Sometimes the militaristic dialect men apply to football becomes so overwrought it's embarrassing. Fox commentator John Madden watched Green Bay Packers assistant coach Gil Haskell being attended to when he got wiped out in a sideline collision during the 1995 playoffs and made this observation on-air: "They're bringing out a stretcher-type device."

During the telecast of an AFL All-Star Game, announcer Curt Gowdy once described a pileup on the field this way: "They're going to have to give some of those players artificial insemination."

Women apply a whole different set of terms to football. For instance, when a man says the Miami Dolphins have blue in their uniforms, she thinks, "No, that's aquamarine." When a player "trots" off the field, she calls it "flouncing" or "sashaying." A man wouldn't dream of using such words. They just aren't built into his inner thesaurus. Football players don't flounce. Scarlett O'Hara flounces. And yet who among us can deny having seen Jerry Rice flounce?

The sexes are only slightly better at understanding each other in the workplace and the household arenas. Women are constantly failing to pick up the power cues of the men at work.

In fact, right there is another perfect example. A guy would never use the phrase "power cue." It's strictly a babe term.

Other babe terms and phrases: processing, relating, projecting, centering, balancing, exchanging, acting out, intimacy, positivism. And when was the last time a guy said, "Do I look fat?"

Guy terms: dissecting, bisecting, assessing, impacting, internalizing, flexing, pumping, chucking, flow chart, paradigm. And how often do we hear a woman say, "Fuckin'-A right, man"?

Perhaps the strain of speaking two completely different languages is why married people become so oblique with each other. They end up not talking at all. The Modern Woman's best friend, Missy, and her husband, Bill the Thrill, have developed an entire system of communication revolving around cooking. It's the language of poultry.

Whenever she cooks a chicken or a turkey, he knows they are going to have sex. She knows that he knows, and he knows that she knows that he knows. It's their way of signaling. So after dinner, he frames a careful reply.

He pours them a couple of Sambucas.

There are some men who find football talk as arid as women do. Former New York Giants running back Herschel Walker says, "It's all just terms and techniques. Once you've got the game, it doesn't change. Block, tackle, run, catch, score. That's all it is."

Jan Wannstedt, who teaches football seminars for women, contends that the language barrier is actually flimsy once you move beyond the initially layer of complexity. "A Bear defense here is a Red Sling there," she says. "It's really just coating, with colors and numbers."

Former Los Angeles Rams stars Fred Dryer and Lance Rentzel mocked the hyperiousness of gridiron chat in a famous incident at Super Bowl IX in 1975, when they posed as a pair of inquiring reporters. They broke up a Pittsburgh Steelers press conference when Rentzel stood and asked unsuspecting head coach Chuck Noll a question.

"Is the zone defense here to stay, and if not, where'd it go?" Rentzel said.

Then they ganged up on Minnesota quarterback Fran Tarkenton. "Strictly off the record, Fran," Dryer said, "is the Super Bowl just another game?"

Tarkenton, enjoying the banter, replied gamely, "I'm just happy to be here."

Dryer followed up: "Is it true, Fran, that you're unable to win the big one?"

Tarkenton grinned. "That's a true statement. I don't have the dedication to come up with the big play in the big game."

Dryer finished by asking Tarkenton what his plans would be if the Vikings won the Super Bowl. "To meet the winner of the Punt, Pass, and Kick contest," Tarkenton said.

The key for women translating football language from malespeak to femalespeak is, when in doubt, to think in terms of war and sex metaphors. They are the Rosetta stones of the game.

A few elementary definitions, in babe parlance:

All-American An honors list for college players, invented by sports columnist Caspar Whitney and Yale coach Walter Camp in 1889, and a tool for the systematic hero-worshipping of nineteen-year-olds.

Assignment Homework. Chore.

Bench Where women have spent the better part of human history.

Blowing Up A trendy phrase used by NFL players to characterize a big hit, as in "I blew him up." Presumably because the loose-limbed appearance of the stricken player resembles something out of *Die Hard II: Die Harder*.

Coin Toss A common practice in collegiate recruiting.

87

Commissioner A corporate tool and licensing flunky.

Concussion The second most oft-spoken word in the NFL, after *"Unnnhhhhh."*

Conference No longer applicable. Formerly, a loose confederation of universities united by geography and common educational philosophies. However, in the early 1990s many conferences were altered by something called "realignment." Schools are now aligned by like-minded greed.

Crackback The male version of backbiting. It is the technique of cutting an opponent's knee out with a sudden reversal and low, sweeping block, usually resulting in catastrophic ligament damage and surgery.

Crouch The way the Grouch sits on the Couch.

Defensive The basic emotional state of the guys in the office.

Draft A human auction established by the NFL in 1935 as a way to distribute players coming out of college. Heisman Trophy winner Jay Berwanger of Chicago, the first player ever chosen, was selected by the Philadelphia Eagles. Teams finishing last pick first, unless they make a trade with another team.

Eligible Available.

Encroachment The precursor to outright harassment.

Face Mask A uniform-type device that they wear on their helmets, so that when they hug each other, they won't come too close to kissing.

Fair Catch Just about the only thing in football that is. When the punt returner raises his hand, it means he will not run with the ball after he catches it. The sole instance in which a player is allowed to field the ball without being hit, and the one time when female spectators can relax.

Feminist Single childless female.

Flooding the Zone It works on the same principle as impregnation. Several receivers run patterns into the same area, overwhelming the defensive coverage. Basically, the idea is that if a lot of little guys all go streaking to the same place, one of them is bound to slip through.

Football A male religious relic, made of four panels of pebble-grained leather, weighing fourteen ounces, filled with twelve ounces of air, retailing for $40.

Formation The style and dress size of the offense: T formation, I formation, wing formation, spread or shotgun formation. As opposed to three-quarter sleeves, double-breasted lapels, and so forth.

Franchise Donna Karan. Ellen Tracy. Tommy Hilfiger. Seattle Seahawks. It's all the same thing, labels and logos, only with cities.

Fundamentals Unfortunately, not reading, writing, and arithmetic, but blocking and tackling.

Gap The emptiness inside since he went away.

Getting Off Quick And they brag about it?

Gridiron The pattern made by the yard lines, which is a copy of an old hot iron.

Halfback A trial separation between the quarterback and running back.

Halftime Show A propaganda exercise, usually executed with supreme tackiness. One part military drill, one part bad Broadway musical, and one part beauty pageant. For many years, thought to be the only portion of a football game women paid attention to. What do they take us for?

Heisman Trophy The statue awarded annually to the Most Popular Boy. The first winner, Jay Berwanger in 1935, was also the first player drafted by the NFL.

Hoopla An old carnival word for a game involving hoops and pegs, now taken to mean the hysterical excitement lavished by men on big games.

Huddle Group therapy for guys.

Kicker The worried little guy in clean clothes who nobody ever talks to because they don't think he's a real jock.

Lateral A sideways or backward toss, usually underhanded, and the only type of movement most women are permitted to make in the corporate structure.

Line of Scrimmage Large men forming piles.

Man in Motion A rare sight when he's home.

Mascot The figurehead identified with a team, most often an animal. As in the Army Mule, the Navy Goat, the LSU Bengal Tiger. A group of New York University students once stole the Fordham Ram. They gave him back a day later. "We just couldn't stand the smell," one said.

Moral Victory Don't let them kid you. Moral, immoral, they'll take it any way they can get it.

NCAA A commercial enterprise not unlike OPEC, under the guise of an educational and athletic association of major colleges, headed by presidents and athletic directors who preach academics with one hand while grabbing for the dough with the other.

NFL A totalitarian regime.

Offensive Frequently in the highest.

Offensive Coordinator The sous chef.

Officials Fat guys in striped shirts, waving hankies. The NFL uses a crew of seven at each game. Their average age is forty-nine and they make anywhere from $300 to $800 a game, depending on years of experience. It's a part-time job, which begs the question of whether they supplement their income on occasion by throwing their calls.

Owners Cranky, meddlesome old men. According to New York Giants co-owner Bob Tisch, one of the few good ones, the only reason to buy into a franchise "is for the ego, and because it makes a nice toy."

Pass Long or short, bullet or feather, it can be welcome or unwelcome, depending on whether you're on offense or defense.

Pattern Designs. Think Mizrahi, Karan, Klein. Crossover, hitch, look-in, swing, screen, out, quick flare.

Play-Action A lie, a deception. The quarterback pretends to hand the ball off when actually he keeps it, so he can either run with it himself, or throw it, or go back out after he leaves you at your front door.

Playbook *The Dead Sea Scrolls.*

Pocket The area where the quarterback lies on his back, trying to regain his senses.

Prevent Defense That stupid weenie strategy coaches use to cover up the fact that their whole team has just gone into the fetal position.

Probation How come nothing ever comes *after* probation in college football? Conventionally, if a violator commits an offense repeatedly, probation is denied. But in the NCAA, probation is the punishment. A school simply goes on probation again and again . . .

Why? Because the NCAA is caught in a dilemma: It must preserve the illusion of propriety and yet does not want to undermine its commercial product with overenforcement of the rules. It therefore follows a course of *selective* discipline.

Program A euphemism for the shady political and financial machinery by which young men with athletic talent are pressed into indentured servitude and subsequently used as human billboards every Saturday afternoon.

Quarter An eternity.

Quarterback A celebrity-type device. The waspy guy who never runs without falling down. Invariably named Jim, John, or Joe.

Receiver A circus performer in tights, and the favorite player of all women. It's the aesthetic.

Recruiting A nationwide hoax.

Sack An ancient concept involving pillaging.

Safety Almost never comes first.

Safety Blitz A sudden lunge by a member of the defense with the express purpose of maiming the opposing quarterback. Babes really get this one, even those who have never played. We don't even need a snap count. We just think of Johnnie Cochran's face.

Salary Cap As if.

Scramble When the waspy guy named Jim, John, or Joe tries to run. Former Miami Dolphins quarterback Bob Griese once lost twenty-nine yards trying to scramble against the Dallas Cowboys. When he finally went down, Bob Lilly said, "This would have been over a lot sooner if you had just cooperated."

Second Effort A last surge by the running back in an attempt to gain the crucial final yard for a first down. Without it, we'd all have cesareans.

Signals The encoded words and numbers that the quarterback uses to tell the offense when to start. He could just say, "One, two, three, go!" but it doesn't sound as good.

Once, the Modern Woman played quarterback in a flag football game and used food for her signals. "Sausage, pepperoni!" she barked. The official stopped her.

"Look," he said, "I don't care what signals you use, but you're making me hungry."

Sky Box A seating-type device and the male mecca.

Snap Very intimate. Very exciting.

Snap Count That tone of voice you use with the kids.

Split End Does it need more explanation than this?

Sweep Running play designed to travel the path of a broom. Like they've ever done it.

Trainer The team medic.

Training Table An eating-type device. The fat man's buffet and the female culinary nightmare. Hunks of meat swimming in oils, steam table vegetables, whole milk, iceberg lettuce with bacon bits and bottled ranch dressing.

Two-Minute Drill Get a drink. Walk the dog. Start dinner. If it says two minutes on the game clock, it will take fifteen minutes on yours.

Upset An emotional disturbance resulting from a romantic reversal.

Varsity A corruption, aptly enough, of the word "university."

Wall Street The one male arena that is even tougher for women to break into than football.

X's and O's A reading-type device for men, with O's representing the offense and X's representing the defense.

the gipper *and other* whoppers

B E H I N D   E V E R Y major disappointment is an unreasonable expectation. And behind every unreasonable expectation is a fairy tale.

There's going to be a man, they tell you.

A man on a horse.

A white horse.

Not a tan one. White.

Not ivory, or bone, or ecru.

White.

If it's a tan one, don't go near it. Don't touch it, don't pet it, don't feed it.

As women grow older, we move into the more elaborately constructed illusions.

There will be a man in a uniform.

With a helmet.

And cleats.

He will have broad shoulders, a tapering waist. From fibula to scapula, perfection.

These fantasies, of course, lead to permanent disenchantment. They all go up in smoke the first time a charm boy holds his cigarette lighter to your heart in high school.

It turns out the guy on the horse won't commit. To anything. He might commit to breakfast or to the Jets game. But that's it. One thing he's definitely not going to commit to is reading you the love poems of John Donne.

He's going to read the paper.

And then he's going to the Y to play pickup.

There is a major misconception going around that women invented fairy tales. Wrong. Guys made them up for the specific purpose of sidetracking us. Guys invented Prince Charming fairy tales to preoccupy and subdue women, so that they could play football. Football is the male version of *The Slipper and the Rose,* a shameless exercise in athletic grandeur and other things that we strident feminist types call Gender Traps.

Guys think that if their team wins, then they've won the Big Contest. Win the game, and they drink the best beer. *All* the best beers. Also, they get the best girl. *All* the best girls.

They get a signing bonus. And they get a giant house on its own cul-de-sac. With a swimming pool, a water slide, a Nerf basketball hoop, a billiards table, a wet bar, several big-screen TVs, and not a single bookshelf. A big sign on the front lawn says: GAME OVER. I WON.

99

And that's just if they win the pickup game.

If they win the Orange Bowl, they get a million dollars, minimum, and if they win the Super Bowl, they get a million-trillion dollars.

Guys believe this, even when they are fifty-five. They still regale you with stories about their athletic feats in the park that afternoon, as if a recruiter is going to ring the doorbell at any moment and offer them scholarships to USC. The reason they are so fervent in their sports fantasies is because they, unlike women, have never been disenchanted.

Women are disabused of their fantasies early on in life. Shortly after our high school boyfriends turn out to be emotional arsonists, we learn that there are things called Domestic Chores, and every babe has to do them, not just Cinderella. No matter how successful a babe becomes, she still has to clean up after someone. Unless she is born with the last name of Radziwell, Grimaldi, Von Bulow, or Cushing. Women with Pamela for a first name also tend to get off.

Whereas guys go on to ever-higher stages of fairytaledom.

This is what all guys think: "I could have played this game if I hadn't blown out my knee."

A quick review of the Disney film library shows that guys made up fairy tales. Disney is how small boys and girls are indoctrinated in Western society. It is the first stage in their intellectual development.

Bambi No mother. Father stud of the forest.

Pinocchio No mother. Two father figures in Gepetto and Jiminy Cricket.

Peter Pan No mother. Doesn't want to grow up. Abducts young woman and makes her sew.

Aladdin No mother. Fortune-hunting tendencies. Likes Princess Jasmine's dough, castle.

The Lion King Has a mother, but he ditches her. Dad's ghost guides him.

Snow White Virgin beauty stalked by evil queen, freed by studly you know who.

Cinderella Evil stepmother. Evil stepsisters. Only hope is studly prince.

Beauty and the Beast No mother. Love interest is a beast, who beneath his beastly getup is a— that's right—studly prince of a guy.

The Little Mermaid No mother. Evil octopus Ursula. Only hope is a studly trans-species prince.

101

Pocahontas Largest-breasted active female on record.

• • •

The next stage in a young man's development is superhero cartoons with toy licensing tie-ins. One spin through Toys "R" Us and every four-year-old in America is certain that all men are built like Tron the Traitorous and are meant to participate in fiery extraterrestrial battles.

Take the Modern Woman's best friend, Missy. One day her seven-year-old, Max, was assigned to draw a picture of Jesus in Sunday school. He really went to work, scrawling with purple crayons all over construction paper.

Then he showed it to her. Jesus was built like something out of a Van Damme movie. Plus he had all this gear.

"What's that on Jesus' belt?" she asked.

"That's his gun, Mommy," he said.

Missy, thinking they were raising a postal office sniper, asked her husband, Bill the Thrill, to spend a little extra time with kid. So the Thrilling One did. And then she overheard this conversation.

"Dad, what's grosser, boogers or snot?"

"Boogers," Bill said.

"Why?" Max asked.

"Because you can throw them at people," Bill said.

• • •

After cartoons, guys graduate to buddy movies, war movies, and demolition flicks. At about six, Dad starts him with *The Fighting Seabees.* Women can't help noticing that there are no equivalent action-type movies for them. One thing that never changes in Hollywood's portrayals of active women is the lunatic sex element. Like Sharon Stone. How come she never plays an undercover agent freeing young American servicemen? Instead her character always has the moral sense of a light switch. She constantly plays kill-happy heiresses or harlots who keep their patience in their diaphrams. Nobody is getting it right, except for Susan Sarandon and sometimes Michelle Pfeiffer, who was pretty good as Catwoman in *Batman Returns,* a dark, sick girl with a body like a whip. "Batman threw me off a roof just when I was starting to feel good about myself," Pfeiffer said. Most active Hollywood females are just visions of nervous men. This is empowered? The convergence of taut muscle, spiritual numbness, and moral blindness?

It's not just Hollywood, either. There are exactly three statues of women in all of New York City: *Mother Goose, Alice in Wonderland,* and *Joan of Arc.*

Anyway, back to guys. A young man's education goes like this: 1) Disney; 2) Violent Weekend Cartoons; and 3) War and Demolition Flicks. Then comes the very last stage in a guy's intellectual development.

Lore.

A man is not fully grown until he has read all of the major sports biographies, as well as the Compleat Works of John R. Tunis and Tex Maule. Ask a guy how many Roosevelts have been President, and he will stare blankly ahead. Ask him how many Super Bowl rings Charles Haley has, and he will spring upright in his chair and say brightly, "Five!"

The Modern Woman has no interest in football lore. She's too busy holding her midlevel job with less pay and less chance of advancement than the modern guy, while also trying to raise two children and choking back her fear that Gilda the daycare center supervisor is a satanic cult worshipper who likes to smear naked little bodies with cat blood.

So when guys start humming fight songs and talking about what a model football is for good old American values and heritage, a siren sounds in the Modern Woman's head like the *"Dive! Dive! Dive!"* alarm on a submarine and a rage seeps into her brain.

Next thing you know, the guy is weeping while he sings the fight songs of schools he didn't even go to, like *On, Brave Old Army Team,* and *The Notre Dame Victory March.* He acts as though he personally sent in the game-winning call in the 1952 Rose Bowl.

A 1992 study at the University of Indiana showed that fans who heavily identify with sports teams regard the successes and failures of the teams as *personal* successes and failures.

Maybe that's why guys perpetuate so many tall tales around football. Heywood Broun noted in 1922 the similarity "between Harvard football and any story by O. Henry."

The problem with lore, as far as the Modern Woman is concerned, is that it is too easily co-opted by people like the Romans and the Nazis and the NCAA. Pretty soon everybody starts believing it and it takes the place of real history.

Give her the real goods.

The Modern Woman is always finding out fascinating little details guys have hidden from her while he was spouting lots of overblown pseudo-historical baloney. She wants a *true* story. For instance, what people from Penn State don't tell you about their famously plain uniforms is that the school colors used to be black and pink.

Their cheer was "Yah! Yah! Yah! Yah! Wish, Wack, Pink, Black!"

No one is more to blame than the Fighting Irish of Notre Dame for perpetuating several dangerous fables and outright whoppers when it comes to football. They are continually swamping the sport in sentiment and false idolatry. Former Fighting Irish linebacker Ned Bolcar used to get teary phone calls in his dorm room from distraught alumni, pleading for him to win for the Gipper. One night before a crucial game against Miami, the so-called outlaw school, Bolcar had to talk down a guy who was having a nervous breakdown right there on the phone. "Hey, man, stop crying," Bolcar said. "We'll win, okay? Just stop crying."

What confuses the Modern Woman is not that men are passionate about football, but that they translate their passions into such outrageous myths and then try to palm them off as truths. Perfectly intelligent men fall for the most obvious kinds of propaganda time and again. Women are more honest about the game. We don't fondly remember the lowest degenerate, simply because he could throw on the run.

Fabled football coach Bob Zuppke of Illinois admitted that a lot of the so-called heroes of the game were media creations. "Show me an All-American, and I'll show you a guy with weak opponents and a poet in the press box," he said. Even Walter Camp, father of modern football and the man who, along with Caspar Whitney, created the All-American team, regretted the hype that was beginning to swamp the game as early as the 1890s. "During the last two or three years, it has become overpopular with the public, and this craze has led it to assume an importance and prominence wholly unsought," Camp complained.

Women have an interesting immunity to the spin-doctoring that occurs around football. We have the capacity to be passionate fans without being fools about it. We do not idealize our sports heroes to nearly the extent that men do. You won't catch the Modern Woman bursting into tears just because she passes Chris Evert in the street. Joan Tisch notes that her husband, Bob Tisch, owns several business interests, the least of which is the New York Giants, but that's all his friends and associates want to talk about. "Not once has anyone said to us, 'How's the insurance business?'" she says.

Female memories are shorter. Not that that is always for the best. Recently, the Modern Woman called Gloria Steinem's office at *Ms.* magazine, hoping to talk to Steinem about the death of Bobby Riggs. A young woman answered the phone in her office.

"Who's Bobby Riggs?" the young woman asked.

Babes don't mind a certain amount of nostalgia. But they would prefer that the pedestals be lowered and the objects of reverence be the slightest bit deserving. When genuine character flaws are whitewashed as boyish foibles, it becomes impossible to tell the good guys from the bad.

107

When a myth gets busted, we're the ones who have to explain it to the kids.

So the next time the guy in the easy chair at home starts waxing lyrical about football, lay a few simple truths on him. Tell him to quit doctoring the past. We can't be spun.

A female reading of some of the taller tales in football:

the four horsemen of notre dame

The truth about Famine, Pestilence, Destruction, and Death is that they averaged five-foot-ten and at least one of them got somebody else to do his homework for him.

They should have been called Three Little Guys and a Real Scholar-Athlete. Their myth was popularized by sportswriter Grantland Rice of *The New York Herald Tribune,* who, after watching the Fighting Irish defeat Army by 13–7 on October 28, 1924, penned this outrageously overwritten paragraph:

"Outlined against a blue-gray October sky, the Four Horsemen rode again. In dramatic lore, they are known as famine, pestilence, destruction, and death. These are only aliases. Their real names are Stuhldreher, Miller, Crowley, and Layden."

Here's the real deal. Quarterback Harry Stuhldreher (five-seven, 151) of Massillon, Ohio, right halfback Don Miller (five-eleven, 160) of Defiance, Ohio, left halfback Jim Crowley (five-eleven, 162) of Green Bay, Wisconsin, and fullback Elmer Layden (six-even, 162) of Davenport, Iowa, were indeed great players, three of them consensus All-Americans, and the core of a national championship team. But they were also small even for the day and beneficiaries of Coach Knute Rockne's savvy public relations sense.

After reading Rice's story, Rockne had a student aide in charge of PR dredge up four plowhorses from the campus farm and pose the players aboard for a famed photograph that immortalized them.

Stuhldreher's classroom performance was recalled this way by Johnny Blood McNally, a star in the pros in the late 1920s and 1930s who spent a brief time at Notre Dame before he got kicked out for overindulging one St. Patrick's Day. "I always like to say that my one contribution at Notre Dame was that I used to write Harry Stuhldreher's English poetry papers for him," McNally said.

the gipper

Among the most famous inspirational speeches of all time was "Win one for the Gipper." Supposedly, when legendary halfback George Gipp of Notre Dame was expiring of pneumonia in 1920, he made a dying request. According to that noted PR firm of Rockne and Rice, Gipp asked that he be baptized by a Notre Dame priest. After he took a communion wafer, he said, "Someday, Rock, sometime, when the going isn't so easy, when the odds are against us, ask a Notre Dame team to win a game for me—for the Gipper. I don't know where I'll be then, Rock, but I'll know about it, and I'll be happy."

According to Rockne, he used Gipp's words at halftime to inspire the Fighting Irish to break a 0–0 tie and go on to victory, 12–6.

But here's another account of the deathbed scene, told by *New York Daily News* writer Paul Gallico. Rockne held Gipp's hand and said, "It must be tough to go, George." To which Gipp replied, "What's tough about it?"

Gipp was a heavy drinker, womanizer, pool hustler, and inveterate gambler who wagered on Notre Dame games. At one point he was expelled, but Rockne pleaded his case to university officials to get Gipp readmitted.

Gallico claimed the truth about Rockne's halftime tearjerkers was that Gipp was no great fan of them. In 1920, when Notre Dame trailed Indiana by ten points at the half, Rockne tried to deliver a rousing speech, but about halfway through he realized Gipp was missing. Afterward, Rockne found Gipp standing at the back door.

Smoking a cigarette.

Gipp told Rockne not to worry, that he had $200 bet on the game. In the second half, Gipp scored two touchdowns.

walter camp

A bloodless, elitist Yalie and the game's first control freak. Walter Camp arrived at Yale as an undergraduate in 1876 and never really left. He dropped out of medical school in favor of a business career, rising to the presidency and board chairmanship of the New Haven Clock Company, which subsidized his passion: the formulating of arcane rules like the system of downs and set yardage and signal-calling. In three ponderous tomes, written in a relentlessly moralizing style, Camp was responsible for advancing the notion that football is a scientific game and based his coaching techniques on a corporate model. Men were cogs or "material" and coaches were autocrats. Camp said it was "entirely inadvisable" to let players know what the outcome of a play should be. He also advised "the whip and spur of continual, and in many cases extremely severe, criticism."

Michael Oriard points out that despite his cerebral posturings, Camp was hardly a civilizing influence. He championed the flying wedge, one of the more brutal tactics ever devised on a playing field. Football, Camp noted, was "an opportunity not afforded in any other sport for the big, overgrown fat boy."

A little-known fact about Walter Camp is that

111

his wife, Allie, served as his de facto assistant coach. Camp had dropped out of Yale after a knee injury ended his football career in 1882 and spent most of his free time loitering around the Yale football field. When his bosses at the New Haven Clock Company objected to his spending afternoons at practice, Walter sent his wife instead.

Allie Camp would watch Yale workouts and scribble in a notebook. In the evenings, she would show them to her husband. Yale star Pudge Heffelfinger remembered that in the 1880s Allie Camp was an integral part of the Eli staff. (Heffelfinger was the first known pro football player, secretly receiving $500 on November 12, 1892, to play for the Allegheny A.A. against the Pittsburgh A.C.)

In John McCallum's book *Ivy League Football Since 1872,* Heffelfinger recalled: "In 1888, Yale actually had two coaches—Camp and his earnest young bride, Allie. They were newlyweds and Walter was sales manager in the New York office of the New Haven Clock Company. His superiors wouldn't let him attend our afternoon practices, so he sent his wife to stand in for him. I can still see her pacing up and down the sideline, taking notes of our scrimmages. Walter kept in touch with our progress by reading her notebook. Then, several nights a week, some of the team would go over to the Camps' home in New Haven for a review of strategy. Allie Camp could spot the good points and the weaknesses in each man's play."

the carlisle indians

The clapboard Indian school in Carlisle, Pennsylvania, was founded by a cavalry officer named R. H. Pratt in an abandoned military barracks as a supposed model of opportunity for young Native Americans. Its most famous graduate was Jim Thorpe. In fact, Carlisle offered only an eighth-grade education at best and its students were forced to hack off their hair, wear secondhand military surplus clothing, and work at menial jobs. "When it comes to educating the Indian, I am a Baptist," Pratt said. "I believe in holding them under until they're immersed." After a good cultural drowning, the Indian youths were then returned to the reservations, where their school experience became extremely problematic. They were shadowland people, not assimilated into either their native tribes or Anglo-Saxon society.

In 1891, a former Carlisle student named Plenty Horses murdered a U.S. cavalry officer, Lieutenant Edward Casey, during the ghost dance uprisings at the Pine Ridge reservation. At his trial, Plenty Horses explained that he committed the murder in an attempt to regain his standing with the Sioux people and "to wipe the stain of Carlisle" from him.

113

Despite its tiny student body, the Carlisle Indians managed to produce some of the greatest upsets in collegiate history, thanks to the coaching of Glenn "Pop" Warner. They had to fight not only the opponents, but referees who showed a decided bias and penchant for cheating them. In 1896, they lost three close games to Harvard, Princeton, and Yale on officiating calls. "We can beat eleven Yale men, but we can't beat eleven Yale men and a Yale referee," Warner complained.

the halftime pep talk

The uninspiring reality is that there is little opportunity for great oratory in the locker room. Rather, teams break up into squads and coaches make dozens of technical adjustments, drawing X's and O's on the chalkboard. "Speeches? Ha!" Dallas Cowboys coach Barry Switzer says. "You're too busy figuring out how to stop this, how to open up that. You're making all kinds of adjustments. Then it's time to go back out on the field. Nobody has *time* for speeches."

you have to be intelligent to play this game

Oh, yeah? Joe Theismann, a former Super Bowl quarterback for the Washington Redskins who is now a TV color commentator, was once asked what the level of intelligence in the NFL was. "There aren't a lot of Norman Einsteins out there," Theismann said.

And how to classify Joe Gibbs, Theismann's former coach? Joe Gibbs was a true football genius, winning Super Bowls with three different quarterbacks. "I considered college a waste of time, except for the people skills I learned," he says. "You learn more from competing in sports than you do sitting in class taking notes."

The author feels compelled to add this public service message to the male youth of America: Boys, only a minute percentage of all college players make it to the NFL. Joe Gibbs, who went to San Diego State, considered only one career alternative to football: stock car racing.

jesus loves you

Guys are always "God"-ing up football. They are always referring to the "cradle" of this and the "temple" of that when they mean Green Bay, Wisconsin, and South Bend, Indiana.

Women believe it is unseemly to apply religion to football. Frankly, such overdramatization is where all the trouble starts. The Modern Woman has been suspicious of prayer in the locker room ever since she read the following in a newspaper: "Gatherers of personal data claim they've found ways to determine what people pray for and that

115

they now know that one out of every twenty-five prays for something bad to happen to somebody."

One year this sign appeared at the First Baptist Church in Fayetteville, Arkansas: FOOTBALL IS ONLY A GAME. SPIRITUAL THINGS ARE ETERNAL. NEVERTHELESS, BEAT TEXAS.

If the Modern Woman was God—a position she feels is not totally out of her range—and some guy took time out of her day to beg for a field goal when there were real wars and famines and such to attend to, it would make her want to wield her lightning bolts like cattle prods.

The Modern Woman feels she could get very good at smiting.

But here is what the Modern Woman really wants to know on the subject of religion and football, being a creature with natural leanings toward procreation: What does it mean to be born . . . again?

paul "bear" bryant

George Blanda once said of Bryant: "That must be what God looks like."

Actually, Bryant's means of winning were quite mortal. When he took over at Alabama, Bryant announced that he was on a five-year plan. "In the first year, a .500 season," he said. "Second year a conference championship. Third year unbeaten, and fourth year national champ."

"What about the fifth year?" someone asked.

"We'll be on probation, of course," Bryant said.

"winning isn't everything. it's the only thing."

Yes, Vince Lombardi said it. The Green Bay Packers coach became known as the General George Patton of football for that statement. But the truth is, he regretted it.

Later Lombardi remarked, "I wish to hell I'd never said that damn thing. I sure as hell didn't mean for people to crush human values and morality."

who let them *in?*

ROBIN ROBERTS, an ESPN and ABC commentator, was hosting an all-female Super Bowl party at her home in Farmington, Connecticut. She carefully placed her centerpiece on the buffet table: not flowers, but a football signed by Troy Aikman.

On a big-screen TV, the Dallas Cowboys and Pittsburgh Steelers ran onto the field. The pregame ceremonies blared out of the set. Things exploded. Smoke wreathed the field.

"Look, terrorists at the Super Bowl," someone said. "And they're going to play anyway. How brave."

In the kitchen, a cluster of women drew up a pool and passed around a hat until it bulged with $150 cash. A debate ensued about whether all of the cash should be awarded to the guest who picked the final score or whether smaller amounts should be awarded after each quarter. They settled on the quarter system.

"That's such a girl thing to do," someone else said. "Guys would make it winner-take-all."

The thing about women sportscasters is that they all know each other. They have had lunch, of course. You might find them in a corner of the local sports bar or at a circular table at the Waldorf, debating the nickel defense or quoting the over-under without once referring to a quarter as "an inning." They are attractive but not glamorous, they are certainly not stupid, and they don't miss a game. They are much like their male colleagues. Frequently, they are better groomed.

They know two speeds on the stove: high and off. They have either very kind husbands or no dates at all—it's hard to find a guy who can pack a shoulder bag quickly enough. Some of them have children, whom they rescue from the hip of the nearest nanny with arresting ease. They range from tall, stately Robin Roberts of ABC and ESPN to the ebullient Andrea Joyce of CBS. They are knowledgeable, funny, and appealing. They have come far from the days when Phyllis George went jogging with George Allen. Or have they, considering the fact that it's the 1990s and no longer fashionable to refer to women as the sex that burns the toast?

The reason women sportscasters all know each other is that there are so few of them. Only a

119

handful of women appear on major network football telecasts, and they are usually relegated to sideline reporting. The evidence suggests that their male colleagues will enjoy far lengthier and better-paid careers. When Phyllis George departed from *The NFL Today* in 1984, she expected to see a procession of women file into the studios. "I'm still watching," she says. "And where are all the women?"

There is a subtle lingering notion that women do not belong in broadcast boothes, press boxes, or locker rooms as critical observers. An exclusive male locker room culture persists.

The locker room is a guy's favorite room in the world. It even finishes ahead of that male mecca, the Den. Men love the locker room because there are hardly any chicks in there. The only ones allowed in are the occasional babe reporters, interviewing players after the Trauma and Spectacle of the Great Contest. The locker room used to be a total No Chicks Zone until 1978. Then babe journalists started suing over discrimination, and carrying microphones and tape recorders and notepads, and asking questions when they should have been writing for beauty magazines. Now the locker room has basically gone the way of fire departments and the Army. It's too bad about the Constitution. The problem with equal rights is that everybody gets them.

• • •

What entitles women to deliver or comment on the sports news, particularly football? Nothing, really, other than the precepts of equal rights and the explosion in the female sports audience in this country over the last twenty-five years. Yet women have encountered a quiet, killing resistance in the major network divisions. Women sportscasters lag not only behind their male colleagues, but behind women in the news and entertainment divisions when it comes to equal pay, prestige, and acceptance.

Hiring and advancement practices have been patently sexist, despite the clear evidence of a burgeoning female audience. Each week between 33 and 40 percent of *Monday Night Football*'s viewership is female, a fact that is virtually ignored by executives and advertisers alike. "It's been sort of this mad conspiracy," says ABC Sports vice president of programming Lydia Stephans. "It's an untapped marketplace."

There might not be any women at all on the air if it weren't for a couple of original thinkers in network positions who suspected a more diverse audience might be out there somewhere. ESPN has been the boldest in assigning significant roles to women. Since 1981, eight women have appeared on *SportsCenter,* including Gayle Gardner and Roberts. Gardner became the first woman sports anchor at a major network when she was hired by NBC in 1988, but after bitter contract disputes with management, she resigned—and went to the Food Network. Former CBS executive producer Ted Shaker lobbied his superiors tirelessly to employ more women before he left CBS in 1993. According to Shaker, it took a lot of convincing, despite the fact that all of the numbers and common sense were on his side. "We were not doing it to make a point," Shaker said at the time. "We were doing it for an audience. But old notions die hard."

Why is it important that the female voice be heard on football telecasts and reports? Because the female football audience has an entirely different and valuable perspective on the game, one that men might find interesting. As it is, women watch football with the sound turned down. That's because most of the announcers are droning former coaches X-ing and O-ing us to death with lengthy discussions about red zones, counters, hitches, slants, and traps.

It is an old adage that male reporters tend to ask a player what the play was, whereas female reporters ask how he *felt* about the play. A generalization maybe, but too often true.

Put more babes in the booth and you'd get a different story. Women talk differently, they interview differently, and they interpret events differently. If one of the heroes on the field screwed up, we wouldn't bury it or launch into a long-winded dissertation on how "he failed to negotiate the safety man." Roberts theorizes that a woman in the booth would include far more information about a player's behavior off the field. "We would definitely quote the rap sheet more," she says.

Putting more women on-air is a double espresso sitting right under the noses of network execs, who refuse to smell the coffee. They fall back on two positions: 1) that women are unqualified, and 2) that the male audience will not accept them. These are nothing but excuses for thinly veiled chauvinism.

Take the issue of personal appearance. The so-called expert football analyst is allowed to be shaggy, overweight, offbeat, or clownish—as long as the person in question is a man. And equal pay for equal work has been a laughable concept. When Gardner in 1991 became the first woman to perform weekly sports anchor duties, she was the highest-paid woman in the business, earning $250,000 a year from NBC. The highest-paid men—Madden, then of CBS, and Al Michaels of ABC—earned upward of $2 million a year. Gardner worked on-air more than any other NBC Sports personality. And yet she earned approximately $100,000 a year less than Charlie Jones and Ahmad Rashad.

"Women are paid equally, and yet they're not,"

123

NBC Sports president Dick Ebersol said at the time. "The few million-dollar salaries are paid to those people whom Madison Avenue pays us to see. When an advertiser buys, he says, 'Is Bob Costas the host of the show?' We don't have advertisers asking us if a woman is the host. That is going to happen someday, but it hasn't happened as yet."

Ebersol went on to predict that by the mid 1990s every network would have a major female star. "The long-awaited revolution and evolution of women in sports television is finally at hand," Ebersol said expansively. He was wrong. The advances have been hiccuping at best.

It is the bedrock position of many men in the business that male audiences want to get their football news from another man—one who has played the game. Agent Ed Hookstratten, who represented Phyllis George, predicts a woman will not succeed at calling play-by-play, the most prestigious assignment in the broadcast booth, until "the guy with the six-pack who wore spikes accepts them."

And yet men accept Bosnian casualty reports from a female news anchor who has never been shot at. "I've never been the President of the United States, either," says ESPN's Lesley Visser.

If men are so uncomfortable with women delivering football news to them, then how to account for the popularity of Robin Roberts, the host who deals out scores, highlights, and news with such credibility? Roberts renegotiated her contracts in the spring of 1995 and came as close as any woman in the business to achieving equal pay, signing for $4 million over six years.

She still lagged a good million or so behind her male peers.

During her tenure as a *SportsCenter* anchor, ratings have increased every single season. Initially, Roberts got a raft of mail from men who wanted her off the air. It slowed to a trickle and then halted, probably in direct relation to her increased experience and confidence in the anchor chair.

Why, then, such obduracy among network decision-makers?

Perhaps, in part, because neither sex is ready yet for the real breakthrough: a female play-by-play analyst. Whether or not we care to admit it, men and women alike remain uncomfortable with the notion of women critiquing male athletic performance.

This is particularly obvious when female reporters enter the locker room. Athletes are used to being lionized or pursued by women, not questioned and viewed dispassionately by them. Especially not when the athletes are nude. It is an unnatural dynamic; normally, such a state of affairs

125

only exists in a strip joint. Men assume that if a football player is naked, a female reporter *must* be looking. "How could she help herself, given the chance to examine such a physical specimen?" he reasons.

At the bottom of the issue is this thought: "Wouldn't a guy look at a naked woman if he had a chance?"

The plain truth is that women do not eroticize the workplace. But try explaining that to the sports-minded man—whether athlete, network exec, team owner, or broadcaster—to whom the refusal of a woman to admire the male physique and athletic prowess may be the ultimate diss.

Which may be why some male athletes insist on flaunting their nudity in locker rooms, instead of simply putting on a towel when a woman enters. The dirty little secret about locker rooms is that men don't have to be naked. They want *to be naked. Locker rooms aren't about privacy—after all, they let cameras in—but about insiders and outsiders and the exclusive fraternity of world-class men. One woman in the business who grew tired of the low-level sexual harassment in the locker room developed a standard response.*

"That looks like a penis," she'd say. "Only smaller."

It's too easy, however, to cry sexism. Women in

126

the industry must take some responsibility for their lack of progress. One problem has been that, as a group, they have tended to be stiff and overly self-conscious. They have muffled their natural voices and abilities in an effort to sound indistinguishable from their male colleagues. When in doubt, they retreat to discussions of medial collaterals rather than risk sounding female.

"I feel like a lot of those women can't be themselves," notes Denver Broncos running back Reggie Rivers. "They've had to project a so-called male personality and ask questions a man would ask."

Too many women have mistaken colorlessness for credibility. Granted, there is no margin for error. Any slip of the tongue by a woman is attributed to her sex, and any flaw in her appearance is judged far more harshly by critics and audiences. Gayle Gardner calls it "the black quarterback syndrome." It is an apt metaphor. What's needed here are a couple of seminal personalities to break old patterns. That means that the women on-air must start taking some chances. They are going to have to be more unashamedly female.

Otherwise, women will continue on the same old marginal treadmill.

In 1987, NBC tried a short-lived experiment, putting sportscaster Gayle Sierens in the booth to call play-by-play. Sierens was capable, but ulti-

127

mately sounded self-conscious, cautious, and discordant. The trial was never repeated. "Truthfully, even I thought it sounded funny," Sierens says.

There are a handful of women working today who are capable of transforming the industry. They have strong, tough, distinctive voices. The question is whether they will get the opportunity.

"Picture a room," Gardner says. "It can be a bar, a fraternity, a living room. And there are thirty men in it, sitting around a television watching football. The door opens, and they turn, and *you* walk in. And you're staying. Here's what they think.

A) Do we really want her here?

B) Can we still do what we usually do?

C) Why would she want to be here anyway?"

Here's what they might answer.

because she has something to prove

Every weekend Robin Roberts's mother turns on the TV to make sure she has chased all of the Mississippi out of her daughter's voice. Sometimes it creeps back in and Lucimarian Roberts picks up the phone and calls Robin in Farmington, Connecticut, to say crisply, "You're getting a little lazy with your *i*'s and your *e*'s again."

Apart from those occasional lapses, Robin

might easily be taken for the product of some tony East Coast school. Her utter correctness on-air makes her seem older than thirty-five. Her rather regal bearing also causes viewers to overlook another fact about her. "I'm dealing with this 'Oh, by the way, I happen to be *black* woman' thing," she says. "An even more exclusive club."

If Robin gets her precise elocution from her mother, who chairs the Mississippi State Board of Education, she gets her erect posture from her father, Lawrence, a retired Air Force colonel. Lawrence was told as a child that they didn't allow black men to fly airplanes. He chose not to believe it and sat in his basement pretending a broom handle was a throttle. Frequently, the Roberts family was the only black one among the officers at the military bases where Lawrence was stationed. The pressure of being a female on-air personality is nothing compared to the pressure of living at an all-white Southern military base, where there was an even smaller margin for error or misbehavior.

Roberts began by working her way through the small radio and television stations of Hammond, Hattiesburg, Biloxi, and Nashville. Frequently, the reply to her tapes was a simple, soul-deadening "You're not what we're looking for." However, by 1988 she was a sports anchor at Atlanta's WAGA-TV. She spent less than two years there before ESPN summoned her. "It's difficult for me to sit here and say, 'Boy, have I been held back,'" she says. "But by my own standards, I was late getting here."

Roberts's next ambition is not a large one. "I just want to stay for a while," she says. "We've never had a woman stay before."

because she's a know-it-all

Lesley Visser is a reformed cheerleader whose hair belongs in Madame Tussaud's and whose voice belongs in a champagne glass. Once an executive told her she was "cosmetically correct" for television. Guys like that have been underestimating her for years. "I don't know if everybody is ready to hear a woman tell them that so-and-so is going to run off left tackle," Visser says. "But you know what? They're going to hear it."

The first time Visser tried to interview Terry Bradshaw—in a stadium tunnel—he grabbed her notepad and signed it. He thought she wanted an autograph.

Years later, Visser would cohost *The NFL Today* with Bradshaw for CBS, the first woman since Phyllis George to appear on the show. Now Bradshaw is a good friend of hers. So is John Madden. That Visser is one of the most engaging women in the business tends to obscure the fact that she is also one of the most knowledgeable. She grew up following the Green Bay Packers, the Boston Celtics, and UCLA. In the sixth grade, she idolized Billie Jean King, Wilma Rudolph, and Auburn halfback Tucker Frederickson. She listened to Muhammad Ali fights on the radio. She memorized backfields. All the things guys did.

In 1976, at the age of twenty-one, Visser became the first female beat writer ever to chronicle an NFL team when she was assigned to cover the New England Patriots for *The Boston Globe.* "I had a migraine the whole year," she says. That a woman suddenly had status as a credentialed observer, operating outside of traditional male-female relationships, didn't sit well with a lot of people. "There weren't a lot of safe harbors," Visser says. "Your fellow staffers resented you, the players thought you were from Mars, and the wives hated you."

Visser spent fourteen years as a daily sports writer for the *Globe* before she accepted an offer from CBS in 1988. Her first season on-air was a painfully public learning experience. She handled the microphone stiffly—"the Ted Baxter of sports," she says—and could not get used to hearing the voices of directors and producers in her earpiece. "I was raised with good manners," she says. "You stop speaking when someone else is talking." Finally Visser is comfortable with her role.

But old notions of proper relationships between men and women aren't dead yet. Visser's televi-

131

sion colleague Howie Long insists on calling her
Lesley Stockton—because she is married to
sportscaster Dick Stockton. Fortunately, she accepts this good-humoredly.

Now Visser has a reply to young women who
approach her and say that they too would love to
go into sports television: "I say, 'Yeah, well, I'd
like to direct.'"

because she's difficult

Gayle Gardner got her first job as a sportscaster
because she hired herself. She got her second job
as a sportscaster because a guy died. "It was not
because everybody was sitting around saying,
'We've got to get this woman on-air,'" she says.

Gardner did not come by her love of sports in
any explicable way. "Reincarnation?" she suggests, shrugging. She grew up in Brooklyn, the
daughter of a liquor salesman and a housewife.
She led a double life: She cut out paper dolls
while watching Y. A. Tittle quarterback the New
York Giants. "It was this closet thing, this other
interest I didn't tell anyone about," she says.

Gardner started as a local talk-show host in Boston and segued into documentary producing. She
became a daily sports anchor at Baltimore's WJZ-
TV in 1983 when her predecessor, Randy Blair,
died of a sudden heart attack.

"Look, I didn't come to this with any particular
cachet," Gardner says. "I was just a person who

grew up in the United States. When I looked around at the people who were sportscasters, I thought they were just people who grew up in the United States too. So I thought, 'Why can't a woman do it?' I just assumed everyone else would think it was a swell idea."

Gardner was the dean of women sportscasters before her troubles began at NBC. Ebersol wanted to use Gardner as a feature reporter. She was adamant that her strength and experience were in anchoring. They never resolved the conflict. "I felt I had worked so hard and so long and fought so hard in the public arena, and I didn't want to lose the credibility I had built doing it," she says.

Gardner grew more and more grim during her stay at the network. Finally she walked away. "In the end," she remarks, "I think you really only get as far as you're allowed to get." Her tenure at NBC was increasingly haunted by the knowledge that she would be expendable as soon as someone decided she was too old, or not attractive enough, or had too much Brooklyn in her accent.

"Can you be a fifty-five-year-old woman sportscaster? We don't know," Gardner says.

because, well, it's kind of a funny story . . .

Andrea Joyce claims that her son, Jake, used to pat the life-sized poster of Michael Jordan that hung in his nursery and call it "Mama."

133

Joyce came late to sportscasting, but she came irrepressibly. She started in television in 1977 as that grand old cliche, a weather bunny. She made $4 an hour watching it snow in Colorado Springs. Then she moved to Wichita for a chance to do the news for $11,000 a year. "Almost as much as a waitress," she says.

As a newscaster for WDIV in her hometown of Detroit, Joyce started hanging around the sports department because she was a loyal Michigan grad who always wanted to know the score. Michigan football coach Bo Schembechler liked to talk to her when he came into the studio to do his weekly show, so she ended up doing bit pieces with him. At WFAA in Dallas, Joyce finally made the full-time switch to sports, weary of spine-aching city council meetings and possessed by the notion that the Texas–Oklahoma game might be more fun.

Joyce's advancement since then has been almost smooth. She moved to New York when her husband, Harry Smith, got his job as coanchor of *CBS This Morning* in 1987. She did some spot work for ESPN and the Madison Square Garden Network before CBS signed her.

There is something soothing about Joyce. She is an able studio host on both college football and basketball. She has also worked on CBS's Olympics coverage. While she may never become the lead woman on a broadcast, she is a valuable re-porter and studio presence whose strength is im-parting information seamlessly. Her smooth de-meanor on-air disguises grueling nights of preparation, up until 3 A.M. reading research files and sports wires. Joyce still calls it the easiest job she's ever had, and it pays well too.

"Me and Harry," she says, "it's not like we live in boxes."

What progress these women have made on-air has come less from the fact that audiences like them than from a grudging sense of obligation among a few wary, pressured executives, most of whom don't actually want them.

"It's the fear of God factor," says agent Art Ka-minsky. "They feel a societal and legal imperative to get women on-air, because networks are hyper-sensitive. They don't want to be called 'anti' any-thing: white, black, left, or right."

But: In the final analysis, networks are most hy-persensitive about money. Financially, male Cau-casians are considered safer bets, particularly at the affiliate level, where news directors are fearful of offending audiences or their superiors by tak-ing chances on young, unproven women. That at-titude creates a self-fulfilling prophecy. Network execs then defend their hiring records by claiming there are no talented or experienced women to choose from.

As of 1990, there were only about 50 women working at 630 affiliates across the country. Consider Lisa Burkhardt's experience at WTVC in Chattanooga, Tennessee. She did straight news for two years after she was told by someone in management that a survey had found that older males in the station's audience would not accept a woman sportscaster.

Burkhardt learned later that viewers had never been polled on that issue.

Even the mildest of network experiments, like Phyllis George's debut on *The NFL Today* in 1975, appears more daring in that light. As Hookstratten describes it, George was "a piece of showmanship" on the part of Bob Wussler, who was president of CBS Sports at the time. "She was never intended to be a sportscaster," Hookstratten says. "She was a personality."

It became fashionable among feminists to regard George as a setback for women. She was too pretty, her work was too soft, her role demeaning. But in retrospect George's role has to be regarded as a major breakthrough. She single-handedly made the female voice acceptable to male viewers. "She went where no one went," Visser says. "And you know what? She was good. Everyone liked her." George made it acceptable for a woman to appear on a Sunday football show. And she did so in the face of hate mail from high school football coaches and open sneering from her male colleagues. "I think I cracked the door," George says. "That's all you could do. I'm not taking any credit. Others pushed it open."

Network execs can argue convincingly that when they are trying to satisfy millions of viewers and protect millions of dollars, they are under no obligation to broaden horizons, particularly if they suspect a female voice might make some male viewers slightly uncomfortable.

But an equally convincing argument can be made that those same decision-makers are getting passed by, failing to cultivate a significant new viewership. Lydia Stephans is one of the few who has grasped that the female sports explosion is an opportunity. She made a significant breakthrough at ABC in 1994 with the launching of the *Passion to Play* series, a feature show on female athletes which demonstrated that there is a whole new ad base to be had.

"A lot of the networks are run predominantly by white males," Stephans says. "Everyone thinks the same. They walk and talk the same. But we're programming for all of these diverse people. You can't assume your audience all grew up white in the Midwest."

Oh, yes, you can. For the moment, sports divi-

137

sions continue to fall farther and farther behind. The most realistic avenues for women are in cable and hard news, where knowledge and diversity—not just white male viewer comfort—have some value. "Comfort is very important," Gardner says. "But you know what? It isn't what makes your existence special, or unusual, or creative. If I was a manager with ten slots open, I would feel it was incumbent on me not to fill them with ten replicas of myself."

While they are waiting for progress, women in the sportscasting business wonder whether it is wiser to agitate or to keep silent. "It's hard enough to do your job and keep the peace," one said. For the time being, they continue to be judged more critically than their male colleagues for what they wear, say, and do; they are given fewer prestigious assignments; and they are paid less. So much for a supposedly enlightened industry.

mothers, studs, *and* *other* menaces

WHEN GUYS talk about the joys of blocking and tackling and how babes may be able to do a lot of things, but by God they can't take a hit, she finds herself saying, "Wanna see my scar?" the way a Hell's Angel offers to show off the knife wounds in his belly. She is tempted to jump to her feet, pull her jeans down into bathing suit country, and display the neat line of a cesarean delivery, which came after twenty hours of labor and consisted of a pain sort of like somebody opening an umbrella down there or maybe a series of crackback blocks, while she begged the doctor—no, implored; no, screamed, really—to get it out. Meanwhile her Rock of a Husband left the delivery room sobbing and when the baby finally was born, it looked like that thing that leaped out of the guy's chest in Alien, *covered in gore. As for her, she had black smears under her eyes, just like that antiglare grease Troy Aikman wears to such great effect.*

The first few weeks he just sort of sat there in

139

his Swing-O-Matic. It was like having a forty-year-old houseguest who kept to himself. She found herself peering down at him, saying, "Is there anything I can get you?"

Then one day he developed this expression on his face like he had just put the cat in the dryer and turned it to the tumble cycle and she knew she was in for trouble. The next day he tried to throw a leg over the crib. She has been playing catch-up ever since.

When the talking began, she learned quickly that the best way to avoid trouble was to converse strictly on a need-to-know basis.

"Mom, can you count to a jillion?" he asked.

"Yeah," she said.

"Do it," he said.

She used to be a good dresser and a reliable phone gossip. Now what she misses most are reasonable conversations. It embarrasses her to talk on the phone. She's always interrupting herself by yelling things like "No fighting on the carpet! Fight on the tile!" Or "You squirt me with that hose one more time and I'll ground you till you start shaving!"

She feels a real twinge when her single friends go out to lunch. She asks them what they ordered and they say, "The cream of broccoli soup and the chicken salad on toast, followed by a frothy little cappuccino." Here's her menu: Chef Boyar-

dee and animal crackers. She tells herself that her single friends are trend-lunching lightweights who live in a completely alternate reality.

He was sweet as a toddler, gentle and full of empathy for all living things. She's sure of it. She distinctly remembers him that way. Then one day his pet frog, Ribbit, hopped into the toilet. There was a lot of screaming and crying. It was a National Tragedy. She tried her best to scoop the frog out with a coffee cup and actually might have saved the poor thing until her husband, the Rock, got into the act. He cleared the bathroom, ordering all women and children into the kitchen. They heard a lot of clattering and clanging. After a while, he strolled back into the kitchen.

"Where is it?" she said.

"I flushed it," he said.

With that her sweet boy burst into delighted laughter and clapped his hands. At that moment, she knew the predator in him had awoken. He ran into the bathroom, where he spent the rest of the afternoon staring with fascination into the Infinity Bowl.

She blames it all on football. When he was six, the Rock entered him in the local PeeWee League. The first day of practice, all these swaggering adult men stood on the sidelines yelling at little boys, who kept chasing butterflies instead of the ball carrier.

141

One coach tossed a football to her son and said, "Don't drop it. That's called choking. Only sissies choke."

Somehow her prince of light managed to catch the thing anyway. She marched out onto the field and not so gently informed the coach that if ever he spoke to her son that way again she would sneak into his house some evening and stage a reenactment of The Burning Bed.

After that the Rock wouldn't let her go to practice or games anymore. He said he was afraid of what would happen if she ever saw anybody actually tackle their son. What he didn't realize is that she would kill anybody who so much as spoke sharply to him.

The part nobody prepared her for was the worry. They didn't warn her about the twenty heart attacks a day she would have to suppress. She can't believe she will get through it without something terrible happening. The older he gets, the more she worries. She feels like a gymnast who gets most of the way through her routine on the balance beam, only to suddenly wobble on the dismount. Of course, there's nothing she can do. She realizes that from the moment he was born, he was out of her hands. The hardest thing in the world for a mother to do is . . . nothing.

142

So when they tell her she doesn't understand football, she just laughs.

What the hell do they think child-rearing is?

• • •

Who is the person football players wave to on the sideline? Zero in on the most aloof NFL star, and he will flap his hands and mouth the words "Hi, Mom!"

Canny college recruiters have learned which parent to make their pitch to. Not Dad. Dad is a cohort, a coconspirator. The decision-maker is Mom.

"Who feeds him?" Hall of Fame coach Bud Wilkinson once said. "Who gives him his dinner? Who's there every Saturday night, watching him on every play? Who comforts him? Who stands by him, whether he wins or loses? If you want to improve morale on a football team, start a mothers' club. She's the heart and soul of your team."

Try telling Barbara Patton that women don't know what it's like in the trenches. Barbara once hit an opposing player so hard she split the woman's helmet. Barbara busted a lot of things wide open in her day, starting with conventional rules of motherhood. Every weekend her son, Marvkus, watched from the bleachers in fascination as his mother went sideline to sideline in full pads for the Los Angeles Dandelions of the National Women's Football League.

It wasn't a bad little precedent in the way of role-modeling. Marvkus would grow up to play in the Super Bowl for the Buffalo Bills before he was traded to the Washington Redskins in 1995.

143

When Marvkus began achieving some renown as a linebacker with the Bills, Barbara worried that his mother's oddball past would embarrass him. It didn't.

"Man, your mother wore sneakers," one of his teammates said.

"No, she didn't," Marvkus said. "She wore cleats."

Barbara wasn't thinking about the feminist politics of the day on that afternoon in 1973 when she heard a radio advertisement for an experimental women's professional football league. "I just wanted to do some hitting," she says.

She called the number and the team's founder, a local electrical contractor named Bob Mathews, told her to come on down for a tryout. At five-foot-three and 130 pounds, she didn't look like the enforcer type, but Barbara was a lifelong football fanatic and all-around athlete who grew up able to hold her own in wrestling matches with her two brothers. She had spent too many afternoons behind chain-link fences, watching her brothers play in empty lots, to resist. "She just enjoyed hitting another girl and knocking her down," her old coach, Bob Edwards, once observed.

Playing for the Dandelions was not recreation. It was a struggle. Barbara had been widowed when her husband, a Los Angeles police officer, was killed in the line of duty. She was single-

144

handedly raising her two children—Marvkus and his older sister, Deborah—while working full-time as an information specialist. Four times a week, Barbara would drive from her office in downtown Los Angeles to her home in Inglewood. She would make dinner for the kids, as well as an occasional nephew or niece, and then turn around and drive them forty miles the other way to Pasadena for football practice.

She earned $25 a game. It was worth it. "It was a pro team, and I was a pro player, and we hit like pros," Barbara says.

The Dandelions practiced four nights a week, with games on Saturdays. Barbara's children would watch practice nightly. Marvkus was five in his mother's first season, too young to know that women weren't supposed to play football. "I don't remember thinking of it as a man's game or a woman's game," he says. "It wasn't an issue. As a kid, you don't think like that." Deborah, on the other hand, did think like that. Years later, she confessed to her mother that she sometimes wanted to look away when Barbara made a tackle.

The Dandelions for a time actually achieved some small local popularity. At their height, they drew two thousand fans. Among Barbara's teammates were a gym teacher, a musician, a secretary, a waitress, a machinist, a mother of three, and a fifty-three-year-old grandmother.

Some women kept their participation a secret.

Others, like Barbara, didn't care. Male coworkers in the office teased her about wearing a helmet. She invited them to the games. "There was this misconception that all women who played football were gay," Barbara says. "Guys would think there was something wrong with a woman who wanted to play football. It wasn't ladylike. Then they would meet you and be surprised that you could be feminine and love football."

On the field, Barbara wasn't exactly Princess Grace. Her coaches marveled at her smash-mouth hitting. Barbara felt transformed in her uniform. "My personality changed out there," she says. She got shaken up a few times, but never had a serious injury.

Barbara and the other players wore full shoulder and hip pads identical to the rig worn by NFL players, with one exception: They added compressed-air pads to their sports bras. "I never did get hurt," Barbara says. "I've gotten hurt worse standing in line in the market when somebody hit me in the breast."

The Dandelions lasted four years. When the team finally floundered in 1976 for lack of funding, Barbara rechanneled her football energies into Marvkus's career. "I'm an entirely different person as a mother," she claims. Well, not entirely. When Marvkus began playing Pop Warner football, Barbara would stand on the sidelines with the fathers, badgering the coaches to put her eight-year-old in the game. "Put my baby in," she would say. "He knows what he's doing."

Barbara was as bad as any guy. By the time Marvkus got to UCLA on a scholarship, he was well on his way to becoming a six-foot-five, 250-pound NFL prospect at linebacker, and Barbara was still badgering coaches to play him more. Marvkus had a decorated career for the Bruins and graduated with a degree in political science with plans to become a lawyer.

While Marvkus was in school in Westwood, it began to get around that his mother had played pro ball. Barbara was sure Marvkus would be embarrassed, but he wasn't. "Actually, I thought it was kind of cool to tell my friends that my mother was a linebacker," Marvkus says.

Barbara is still trying to coach him. Her favorite times are when Marvkus comes home to L.A. and they can go over taped replays together. Barbara just hates it when he arm tackles. "You won't catch anybody that way," she says. Occasionally, she makes a good point, although she has fallen behind on some of the more sophisticated terminology.

"I try to remind her that I am a professional football player," Marvkus says. "And then she tells me that she was one too."

What is the difference between a mother and a coach? Nothing, really. Both are despots on the level of Napoleon. Both are control freaks accustomed to issuing commands and being obeyed without question. Women understand the dynamics of player-coach relationships. Mothers have been coaching their children for years.

Mom comes to visit and suddenly the silverware moves from one drawer to another. "It should go by the sink," she says. Whole rooms full of furniture shift. Things disappear and other things appear in their place. For the ability to bend other people to her will, there is no one like Mom. Without ever putting down her nail file, she can command an entire family.

"I'm your mother," is all she has to say.

"You're a midget," we are tempted to reply.

Joyce Scott can be credited with helping to save the career of her son, Darnay Scott, a receiver with the Cincinnati Bengals. Darnay did not endear himself to his coaching staff in 1994 when he showed up for minicamp hopelessly out of shape. Quarterback Jeff Blake had to hector him through wind sprints.

"If he wants to play himself out of the league in two, three years, he's doing it," Coach Dave Shula said, infuriated.

When Joyce heard about her son's poor conditioning, she got him on the phone from her home in San Diego. Darnay complained about how sore he was and said he was going to skip the voluntary camp in May.

148

"I'll tell you what. You get on the next plane and come home," Joyce said.

Joyce took charge of her son's training. She woke Darnay up every day at 7 A.M. and chased him outside for a run. Then she supervised his gym workout. "She got me taking care of business," Darnay said. When he returned to the Bengals, he wasn't ready for a marathon, but he was considerably better than he had been.

"I love her," Shula said.

Perhaps the most common female experience in football is that of a mother, sitting in the grandstand at her son's game. If you want to see total female aggression, just go to any Pop Warner game and watch the mothers. The most mortifying experience of 49er quarterback Steve Young's life occurred on a fall afternoon when he was a boy. He told the story to Michael Silver of *Sports Illustrated:* He got hit in the middle of a game and rose from the turf to see his mother, Shari, charging out of the stands.

Shari grabbed the opposing player by the neck and started shaking him. "Don't you *ever* hit my son like that again!" she yelled.

Steve, furious, started hollering back at his mother. "Get out of here!" he said. "You're a woman! Don't you understand? It's a privilege for you to be here!"

Steve Young says that to this day he insists that

149

his mother sit as high up in the stadium as possible. He's afraid she might do it again. "You," he orders her, "up in the bleachers!"

What Young doesn't understand is that motherhood is to women what football is to men. It is our greatest metaphor and passion. It is our version of slugging it out in the mud. It is our female bonding ritual. It is our lesson in character building, in absorbing great victories and devastating losses. And it is our version of ritual public humiliation.

part three

MEN
will be
BOYS

On a raw Saturday in October, a team named Heat on Ice gathered on a muddy weed-strewn field at Fort Hamilton High School in Brooklyn, New York. They piled their coats and bags on the ground. Somebody set down a toolbox next to a purse.

They stretched and buckled on the plastic belts that hold the "flags," colored strips of cloth.

Suddenly a woman screamed.

The Heat scattered, grabbing up their coats and mouth guards. They stared at the ground.

It was a worm.

After order was restored, quarterback Andra Douglas began working out a pattern with receiver Theresa Primus. Douglas, a corporate art director, scratched out something in the dirt.

She dubbed the play Bird Beak.

"That's what it looks like," she said, studying her diagram in the dust. "A redbird's beak."

Douglas started playing football with the neigh-

153

borhood boys in Zephyr Hills, Florida, the rural suburb of Tampa where she grew up. She was the fastest kid in high school, a skinny blond metabolic miracle, able to outrun most of the local varsity high school team. Some of the guys even petitioned the head coach to let her try out for the team, but he refused.

"There was never going to be anything athletic I could pursue as a career," she says. "I had to sit and watch while all the guys I could beat in a footrace got scholarships and walked into stadiums."

Instead, Douglas went to Florida State and became a star for the women's rugby club. She played wing and outside center on a team that won back-to-back club sport national championships in 1980–81. When she graduated, she would not get another chance to play competitively until she discovered the Brooklyn flag football league.

Once Douglas asked a game official if there was any difference between the flag football games he officiated and the men's games. "Yeah," he said. "The women smell better."

They also wear more jewelry. Heat on Ice co-captain Valerie Oliver, a corrections officer, called the team together. "Okay, ladies, give it up," she said.

The women began removing their earrings, necklaces, and bracelets. A heap of gold and silver baubles grew steadily higher. A woman named Shana Krooms took longer than the others; she had seven earrings in one ear alone. Rachel Wilson, another cocaptain, inspected Krooms. She gestured at her, rolling her eyes.

Reluctantly, Krooms removed her nose stud.

Wilson led a prayer circle. "Lord, give us the strength to play hard and play safely," she said. "Okay. Now let's kick up on these girls' butts."

They broke and drifted to the sideline. As the game got under way, Krooms surveyed the enemy, the Bulldogs.

"Blue jerseys with orange flags," she announced, shaking her head. "Look at that. Fashion Police. I'm issuing a ticket. Go directly to Nine West."

Douglas completed a quick out pass to a receiver named Tracy Smitherman, who sprinted up the Heat sideline. As she was about to get her flag pulled, she lateraled to Oliver, but Oliver fumbled it out of bounds.

"Oh, Val, you suck!" Oliver screamed.

Teammate Bernadette Hamilton glared at Oliver.

"Give me twenty," she said.

Oliver dropped to the ground and pumped out twenty push-ups.

"Somebody put a chair on her ass," said Primus.

Center Anna Tate, nicknamed Tonka, a well-muscled woman with a special talent for pancaking, flattened an opponent as Douglas gathered in a kickoff. Douglas used the block to spring to the outside and raced for a touchdown. On the sideline, Connie Edwards applauded wildly.

"Look at her knock that girl down," she said. "I wish I could do that. I drink milk. Nothing happens."

The Heat won, 20–12. Afterward they gathered around Oliver again, this time to conduct a few pieces of administrative business. "Ladies," she announced, "I need three dollars apiece from you for a new football."

Douglas pulled on her coat, giggling. She was remembering another, similar occasion, when a woman had grown frustrated with all the talk and uttered a statement now famous in Brooklyn flag football annals.

The impatient, high-pitched voice had rung out across the field.

"Let's go!" the voice called. "The wives are at the bar!"

dressing down

WOMEN KNOW from decorative. We have always suspected that there is a good deal more fashion than function in football gear. An informal survey of college and NFL players confirms this—and reveals that there is as much vanity, pretension, and neuroticism in a football dressing room as there is in a Bergdorf Goodman changing cubicle.

When it comes to the care and clothing of their bodies, football players show us their most feminine side—ironically, just when they are trying to look their most masculine. Beneath the pads they like delicate fabrics, skin moisturizers, and all-natural cottons as much as the next girl.

Miami Dolphins quarterback Dan Marino blew their cover years ago, when a reporter asked him why he wore double layers of sweatbands on his wrists. Marino refused to reply to the question. The reporter persisted.

"Why two sweatbands?" he asked.

"Because it looks good, all right?" Marino said.

Donna Karan has seen you for what you are all along. According to Karan, an NFL uniform is not that far removed from some of her own designs. "There's a sensual shape to it," Karan told an NFL Films crew. "The leggings. The shirt with the padding. It's the bodysuit I've been trying to get men into for years."

Clothing, as any woman knows, is a statement of self-image. So what does it say that all men love gear? It says that they enjoy playing dress-up, and they always have—they just haven't been permitted to express it.

They concentrate instead on their sports uniforms. Camping vests. Military habiliments. French Impressionist painter Berthe Morisot wryly noted this dandyish tendency in her colleague and future brother-in-law, Édouard Manet, during the Franco-Prussian War.

"Édouard," she wrote, "spent most of the war changing his uniform."

Not only do all men love gear, they are obsessed with it. This explains the electronic revolving tie rack. One time the Modern Woman's best friend, Missy, and her husband, Bill the Thrill, decided to take the kids on a camping weekend. Bill had a field day buying gear. Fur-hooded parkas. Nylon pants. Snowshoes. Skis. And $5,000 in new luggage. All for a two-day trip.

"Excuse me," Missy said. *"When did you enter us in the Iditarod?"*

There are two practical purposes for a uniform: to tell one team from the other and to protect the various body parts from injury. The rest is all adornment. It is a sign of just how much of football dress is affectation and aesthetic that most college and pro players do not bother to wear protective cups.

Would anyone go so far as to argue that football pants serve an actual purpose? "Those tight little pants that show their butts are nothing but vanity," says Colleen Coley, seamstress and laundress to the Dallas Cowboys, who hand-alters their clothes.

Football players dress with three things in mind, in the following order: image, superstition, and function. Many men feel, rightly, that the three are intertwined. In order to play like a star, they must *feel* like one. "The first obligation of a football player is to look right," former Heisman Trophy winner Doug Flutie once said.

That must be why so many players wear jewelry on the field. Dallas Cowboys running back Emmitt Smith will not let equipment managers remove the diamond stud from his ear until after the National Anthem.

159

"It's like a gladiator going out to do battle," Phil Simms says. "You want to make sure your armor and your garments are in order. And yes, everyone wants to looks good too."

It is a source of endless amusement to locker-room staffs across the country that players will linger in the dressing room until the last minute, moussing their hair, only to put on their helmets when they jog onto the field. The interior of any player's locker includes an array of hair- and skin-care products, gels, brushes, skin creams. Herschel Walker, the very definition of masculinity, has a particularly dainty postgame ritual. In the course of a casual conversation with the press after practice, Walker applies his aftershave and several layers of Vaseline Intensive Care. Next, he applies his facial moisturizer. Then a hand cream. Finally he rubs little dabs of Vaseline into his fingertips.

When St. Louis Rams equipment manager Todd Hewitt applied eye black to the face of former quarterback Jim Everett, Everett would ask, "Is it straight?"

At the University of Oklahoma, equipment manager David Littlejohn finally put up two large mirrors, one at each end of the locker room, because players were always jockeying for position to study themselves. "If they all worried as much about how they played as how they looked, there would be a lot more good teams out there," Littlejohn says.

Dallas Cowboys defensive back/wide receiver

Deion Sanders is perhaps the best-known Beau Brummell in the league—as well as one of the more meticulously superstitious. Before a game, Sanders lays every article of his uniform out flat on the floor, from his socks all the way to his headband. Then he begins to dress himself in reverse order, working from the toes up.

Some players start their grooming long before the game. "You see it on the team plane," says Pittsburgh running back Jerome Bettis. "Guys start shining their shoes. You're trying to get in a frame of mind for what you're going to do on the field. And it depends on who you're going to play. If you're going to New York, it's different than Carolina. You want to spruce up, have that little extra bit of tidiness."

The NFL is so concerned with appearances that it sends officials to every game for the sole purpose of guarding against untucked shirts, non-regulation articles of clothing, and other violations of its many dressing rules. League officials are no fools; they are well aware that the figures cut by the players are pleasing to the public eye and are worth a fortune in licensing and concession sales. But that doesn't stop players from indulging their idiosyncrasies and peccadilloes.

Phil Simms once got fined $1,500 for pulling his socks up too high. An illegally large waist towel can draw a $5,000 fine.

Jerry Rice, the receiver beyond compare for the

San Francisco 49ers, spats his shoes. Spatting is the popular practice of winding tape around the middle of the cleat. Many players feel the tape makes their shoes more stable. "But mostly guys just think it's cool," Todd Hewitt says.

Football players are crimped, curled, girdled, and yet ineffably male. Notice the team colors. No muted effeminate bottle greens, no camels, no grays. We're talking bold and bright. The cut is streamlined. No naughty drop shoulders, no pleats, no soft folds (except of fat).

Fashions, of course, change. They are dictated by the players themselves, who have begun to heavily alter their garments to suit their personal styles.

Some tips for the well-dressed football man:

the jersey

Cuffed sleeves or loose? Cropped waist or long? It all depends on what image the gentleman wishes to project. The most up-to-date lineman wears oversized shoulder pads and a jersey altered to the choking point, à la Cowboy Erik Williams. Tightness is both becoming and pragmatic: It makes it difficult for the opposition to gain any purchase with their hands and helps disguise the size of the gut.

If the gentleman wishes to be truly cutting edge, he should wear an extremely short, cuffed sleeve.

The cuffs are very *au courant,* à la Emmitt Smith. Players prefer them because they allow maximum view of the bicep and tricep. "They sort of pinch your muscle, so it pushes it up," Denver Broncos running back Reggie Rivers says. The cuffed elastic strip gently causes the muscle to distend, without discomfort.

This is known in the NFL as "showing your guns."

the neckline

Whether scoop-necked or V, throw caution and practical considerations to the wind.

Some players tailor their jerseys so severely they no longer resemble recognizable human articles. During the 1995 season, a St. Louis team executive asked for a cast-off jersey of receiver Todd Kinchen's to give to his son. A day later the executive returned it. It was too small. The kid couldn't get it on.

One method of entry is to pull the jersey over the pads first. With the help of two men, the whole housing can then be hauled on and off the torso. This can make pulling on a pair of boots seem like child's play. "I have a real respect for women trying to put on panty hose," Todd Hewitt says.

A warning. Excessive tightness can cause problems. Players have been known to complain of constricted breathing and even anxiety attacks. Ex-Ram Bill Bain, a 300-pound guard, suffered from claustrophobia. When the equipment staff would try to put him into his pads and jersey, he would get dry heaves.

Once, just prior to a big game against the 49ers, Bain panicked as the jersey and pads settled over his head.

"Get it off me, get it off me!" Bain screamed and threw the jersey across the room.

Hewitt loosened the stitching, and Bain finally made it out to the field.

Quarterbacks like Troy Aikman require a looser, more flowing look to allow freedom of movement. "Quarterbacks are the most finicky and fashion-conscious," Oklahoma's Littlejohn says. "They'll want a certain-size shoulder pad, but a jersey with a certain type of body and a certain type of openings in it. It's all got to be positioned just right, down to the sweatbands. Then the game starts and it all goes out the window."

Receivers also prefer a more flowing jersey. Michael Irvin demanded a larger, longer sleeve. But not solely because it made it easier for him to catch the ball. "He thinks his arms are small, so he likes to hide them," Dallas equipment manager Mike McCord says.

Receivers and defensive backs tend to be minimalists. Deion Sanders does not like to have anything tucked into his pants. However, NFL rules require that all players tuck in their shirts. So Sanders has his jersey tailored and tapered to exactly meet his belt line, creating a seamless effect that *looks* like he is tucked in.

the pants

For the ultimate in sophistication, there is really nothing like a well-cut trouser.

Football pants are nothing more than Lycra tights, with built-in compartments for padding. On a hanger, they look like dolls' clothes. The trend of the moment is to wear them as small as possible, so when they are pulled on they fit like Danskin. Players who want the utmost in cling demand a new pair every two weeks, as they lose much of their elasticity after a hard Sunday. Simms used to put his pants on an hour before game time, because that's how long it took to stretch them out.

Rams linebacker Shane Conlan is six-foot-three and 240 pounds—and wears size 32 short. "They want the snugness," Hewitt says. "But, really, it's the look they're trying to accomplish." The Rams' Darryl Henley used to wear 26s—and roll the waist of his pants over, trying to get them to fit even tighter. Finally he asked Hewitt for a pair of 24s. He said the 26s just didn't look good.

"Maybe I can get some from a Pop Warner league," Hewitt told him.

Finally Hewitt had a pair of extra-short 24s custom-made. "My nine-year-old couldn't get into them," Hewitt said. Henley loved them.

the pads

The basic equipment consists of shoulder, hip, thigh, and tailbone pads. Pads are generally more for practicality than appearance, but even they follow some fashion trends. Take the neck roll. It was originally designed to be worn close behind the neck to prevent spinal injuries, but players prefer to wear it settled back around the shoulders—where it does absolutely no good at all.

The size of padding varies greatly. For those interested in an elegant but not overstated enhancement of the male physique, there are any number of attractive options. At Oklahoma, David Littlejohn keeps eight different sizes of thigh pads available, ranging in size and weight.

Four of those styles weigh just ounces. Even then, some guys complain they are too heavy. Littlejohn just grins.

"Son, if that's too heavy, then you're in the wrong sport," he says.

Much as women enjoy the fashion aesthetic of football, however, it is spoiled by an ugly thought.

Who does all that laundry?

It would not occur to most guys to wonder who is in charge of cleaning and mending for a football team. But to babes, it is a burning issue. A pro team carries a roster of fifty-three active players. During the season, it takes an average 1,500 pounds of laundry a day to keep a team in clean sweats and towels. College is worse. At the University of Oklahoma, the Sooners go through 2,500 pounds a day.

Somebody has to pick up after them.

"We're the mothers of the organization," says Dallas manager Mike McCord. "We do every thankless task. We pack for them, we clean up after them. If we didn't, they'd show up with two left shoes."

Every Monday morning Colleen Coley pulls her mommy van up to the back door of the Dallas Cowboys complex in Valley Ranch, Texas, and loads a hamper full of blue-gray, star-shouldered uniforms, habiliments so light in texture that they could be mistaken for lingerie. The satiny glamorous appearance of America's Team rests solely in the tired and somewhat chapped hands of this thirty-three-year-old suburban mother of three, who darns and cleans the Cowboys' fifty-three uniforms each week out of her laundry room at home.

"Our lady," as Aikman, Smith, and company refer to her, puts in fifty hours a week scrubbing

167

and patching, only to cheerfully watch her handiwork get pulled to pieces again on Sunday. One time Nate Newton, the Cowboys' hulking 325-pound lineman, watched Miss Colleen and Mike McCord load a heavy hamper full of Cowboys gear into her van, which has been customized so it can comfortably hold the team's laundry along with her three kids.

"Damn, Miss Colleen's stronger than you are, Mike," Newton said.

Miss Colleen swung a bag of coaches' dry cleaning at Newton. "Watch out, Nate," she said, "or I'll shrink your pants."

Miss Colleen is devoted to the Cowboys. She puts almost as much care into their uniforms as she does into the care and feeding of her children: Priscilla, eight; Martin, three; and Chelby, two. So much so that she conceived Martin and Chelby on successive Super Bowl Sundays, in celebration of the Cowboys' back-to-back victories.

It seems Miss Colleen and her husband, Kevin, a printer, got a little carried away on tequila and decided to give the fighting men on the field a real salute.

Miss Colleen likes to think Martin and Chelby have been doing their bit for the Cowboys since they were in the womb. They each managed to get themselves born during bye weeks in the fall schedule, so Colleen had seven whole days after each birth to recuperate before she had to start doing the team's laundry again. "It was a real concern," she said.

The laundering of America's Team is no simple matter. In Miss Colleen's utility room, three washers with stainless-steel drums line a wall. She has rigged them with cold-only water lines, so there is no danger of hot water leaking in and making the colors run, the numbers peel, or the more delicate fabrics spoil.

After seven years as laundress and seamstress to the team, Miss Colleen knows the physical dimensions and personal habits of every veteran Cowboy. Each fall the players line up while she takes in or lets out their pants, raises or lowers the hemlines on their jerseys, adds darts or takes them away. She tapers here, tailors there.

Every Monday Miss Colleen goes through the uniforms with a needle and thread and a variety of industrial cleaning chemicals and home remedies. Usually she uses a store-bought detergent for the regular loads, but she is creative with the tougher, more unusual stains.

Miss Colleen's biggest problems are the individual peccadilloes of the players. Emmitt Smith holds the ball so tightly to his sweating body when he runs that the leather coating and red NFL logo have left an indelible mark in the midriff area of his jersey, which is also rent by tears

169

and claw marks caused by opposing defenses. Miss Colleen has tried everything, but the faint reddish outline of the ball remains. By the 1995 Super Bowl, Smith was in his fourth jersey of the season.

"You don't notice it on TV, but his front is slightly pink," she says.

Special teams captain Bill Bates's jersey is always among the worst. He has small holes all over his front, where the face masks of opposing players have caught in the mesh. Defensive star Charles Haley's jersey is another problem. He refuses to wear newer models until he absolutely has to, preferring his old worn-thin jersey, inventively repaired by Miss Colleen, until it practically falls off his shoulders.

Newton insists that Miss Colleen darn the same pair of socks by hand, rather than simply getting a new pair from the well-stocked shelves.

Aikman refuses to wear a chin pad. "And every year he busts his chin wide open," Miss Colleen says. "Then he wipes the blood off with his jersey." By the third game of the 1995 season, Aikman needed a new jersey because Miss Colleen couldn't get the stains out. Aikman agreed to wear a chin pad.

Deion Sanders almost ruined his jersey in his very first game as a Dallas Cowboy on October 29, 1995, a 28–13 victory over the Atlanta Falcons. It was late in the game and Sanders, the two-way threat, made a star turn at wide receiver. He streaked toward the end zone on a post pattern and Aikman heaved a bomb. Sanders made a theatrical leap for the ball, just missing it, and slid on his belly across the artificial turf, sustaining what is known as the "big burn." A giant raw strawberry blossomed across his stomach, bleeding into the brand-new jersey.

By the time Miss Colleen got to the shirt, at about 1 P.M. the following Monday, it was stiff with dried blood. An assortment of industrial chemicals did nothing. Finally she tried some Liquid Dawn. The blood lifted. She counts it as one of her greatest triumphs.

"You'd be amazed at the things I can come up with," Miss Colleen boasts. "There's not but one thing I can't get out."

What's that?

"Orange Gatorade."

deadly testosterone buildup

EXCERPTED FROM the *Journal for the Study of Sports Pathology:*

Researchers this week announced the discovery of a previously undiagnosed disease that is afflicting some of the nation's most popular sports figures. Have a nasty encounter with an armed-to-the-teeth Pro Bowler? Don't rush to judgment. Scientists now say the perpetrator may well be suffering from Deadly Testosterone Buildup (DTB), the abnormal proliferation of androgens that is striking football players in disproportionate numbers.

Previously, hyperaggression in football players that resulted in violence was thought to stem from involvement in a sport requiring extreme physical contact. But researchers now concede they may have been in error. While the exact pathology of Deadly Testosterone Buildup remains obscure and hotly debated, the word "no" appears to have a particularly explosive effect on sufferers.

Although the chief manifestation of Deadly Testosterone Buildup is the expression of violence, particularly toward women, researchers have already documented several subsidiary effects, ranging from selective blindness to a propensity to lead a double life. "In one instance, the mustache of a prominent NFL veteran quite literally exploded off his face and stuck to the opposite wall during clinical evaluation," said Dr. Ari Stetmer, the leading researcher in the field.

A handful of scientists now believe that Adolf Hitler, Catherine the Great, and composer Richard Wagner may have suffered from the insidious affliction. But by far the most convincing evidence to date of the disease's existence comes from that potentially misunderstood figure: O. J. Simpson. Indeed, researchers believe Simpson may someday be to Deadly Testosterone Buildup what Lou Gehrig was to Lou Gehrig's disease.

"We may name it after him," Stetmer says.

The sudden withdrawal of adulation, particularly when exacerbated by the presence in the bloodstream of alchohol or drugs, such as steroids, cocaine, or crystal meth, is what most often triggers the disease, according to Stetmer. Hormonal imbalances flood the body, rising steadily until they reach eyeball level (accounting for severe blind spots), and then continue to the brain, at which point the result is a lashing out.

Although physicians are just beginning to

gather data on the new scourge, they already fear that, unchecked, the disease may mean that some of the most highly regarded players in the NFL could someday require institutionalization.

"I'm afraid that at a certain point it's like trying to teach table manners to a *Tyrannosaurus rex*," says Stetmer.

Researchers had the opportunity to study the effects of DTB up close when a particularly virulent incidence of it broke out at Midwestern University, the legendary football power and pride of the Wheat Belt. In October of 1998 Heisman Trophy candidate Sorence Chillups was arrested for assaulting his former girlfriend, undergraduate Brenda Jean McCall, as she studied in the campus library.

It was his seventh attack on McCall since she ended their relationship three months earlier. Chillups pled no contest to aggravated assault. Judge Bob Throckmorton, a Midwestern alumnus, sentenced him to undergo a mandatory one-hour counseling program.

Asked on the courthouse steps if he had anything to say, Chillups replied, "I am the real victim here."

Midwestern coach Tom Oldman refused to suspend Chillups from the team, despite nationwide calls for additional disciplinary action.

174

"Are you kidding? Have you seen him run with the ball?" Oldman said.

Oldman came under further attack when he started Chillups in the Hooters Hula Bowl. Chillups led the Corndogs to a 42–7 victory over USC, rushing for 225 yards and six touchdowns. Asked if he had any reaction to the outraged demands for his dismissal by the National Organization for Women, Oldman said, "It's time these feminist groups lost their spoiled-brat mentality."

Said Chillups's best friend and teammate, defensive tackle Brent "Stormdrain" Bottoms, "What was that babe doing in the library anyway? If she was really afraid of him, she would have left school."

But the story took yet another twist two days later, when McCall sprang from a cheering crowd to attack Chillups as he disembarked from the team plane. Witnesses said McCall, a six-foot-two, 145-pound forward on the Lady Doggers basketball team, doubled Chillups over with a fist to the stomach and then pulled a socket wrench from her letter jacket and began hammering at him.

"God, it was awful. She kicked the living shit out of him," Bottoms said, sobbing. Bottoms added that he was stunned to hear some females in the crowd urge McCall on.

McCall was arraigned on a charge of aggravated assault. "Absolutely 100 percent guilty," she said, when asked by Judge Throckmorton how she pleaded.

175

McCall was sentenced to two years in prison.

Asked for his reaction, Chillups found it impossible to respond through his wired jaw.

Researchers now believe that Chillups was indeed a victim—of DTB. Stetmer says Chillups showed the classic signs: a spotless reputation conflicting with his actual character, superstar status coupled with a permissive environment, and a blazing publicity campaign on his behalf.

Stetmer maintains that in light of the Chillups case, work previously regarded as groundbreaking in the study of athletes and violence must now be discounted as "completely off-base." He was referring specifically to a 1995 study of college campuses that showed that athletes were slightly more likely to be reported for violent crimes against women than the regular student body.

"Statistics, schmatistics," Stetmer says. "Look. What do you expect? He's treated as a star everywhere he goes, his ego and his testosterone skyrocket, and everybody fawns over him. Except for the girl, who sees him for who he really is. So he sets out to get her. Big surprise there."

Since the announcement confirming the existence of DTB, researchers have begun to feverishly rethink the Simpson trial. Piles of transcripts and depositions line the hallways of the DTB Center, a modern antiseptic structure in Bristol, Connecticut, not a stone's throw from ESPN headquarters.

"Well, what's clear is that they bungled the case," says Dr. Benny Dict, an associate of Stetmer's in charge of marshaling Simpson DTB data.

Dict goes out on a limb where his colleagues are not yet willing to go and suggests that DTB could be contagious. In fact, Dict believes that Simpson's entire defense team may have been infected by the disease. What does he offer as evidence? "In a nutshell, Johnnie Cochran," he says.

Dict asserts that the presence of DTB on the defense team is all the more certain in his mind given Cochran's penchant for touching Simpson, coupled with the fact that there was absolutely no sign of testosterone in either the prosecution or in Judge Lance Ito. "Hah. If only," said Denise Brown, sister of the deceased Nicole Brown Simpson.

Who, other than football players, does DTB strike? Stetmer does not rule out any celebrity who shows a pattern of contradictory behavior. Indeed, he became convinced of DTB's existence while watching the Grammy Awards, when Crosby, Stills, and Nash appeared wearing red AIDS ribbons and sang *Love the One You're With*.

Tragically, virtually every male sportscaster displays DTB symptoms. One notable exception was Howard Cosell, the only man who seemed to see through Simpson's facade while the rest of his colleagues slavered over the Hall of Fame running back. "That little lost boy" Cosell called him.

Can DTB occur in children? In extreme circumstances, yes. "I would keep a pretty sharp eye on Cody Gifford," Stetmer says.

How should loved ones deal with DTB sufferers? Accede to all of their wishes, Stetmer advises, and under no circumstances reject them sexually.

"The most pressing question is: Should women fear football players?" Stetmer continued. "I can answer definitively: No. Not unless they date them."

Does Deadly Testosterone Buildup exist? A quick perusal of the sports section on any given day would suggest that it does. Sometimes we wonder if there is anyone left in the NFL who *hasn't* been accused of assaulting a woman. Twelve Cincinnati Bengals at a time. Eight Denver Broncos. Three Oakland Raiders.

Go directly to the source and ask a football player whether his ilk is more prone to commit crimes of violence against women, be it gang rape, date rape, or domestic abuse, and he will tremble at the unfairness of it all. Thousands upon thousands of rapes and assaults by nonathletes go unreported by the media, he will tell you, yet every single alleged attack by a football player makes a headline, creating a twisted image of rapacious gridiron savages. First, there was the dumb jock stereotype and now there is the misogynist jock.

"In certain football players, violent tendencies are going to be there, whether they play the game or not," says Boomer Esiason. "Does football accentuate that behavior off the field? No. It's about the person, not the sport. There is such a hodgepodge in this league. There are some of the dumbest guys in the world and some of the smartest guys in the world. You'll find that 98 percent of the men in the NFL are gentlemen who treat women and their families with great respect. It's an unfortunate stereotype."

Unfortunately, there are no categorical answers to the question: Should women fear football players? Only since the late 1980s has rigorous study been done on the subject and the press has frequently misinterpreted or overstated data. Some of it indicates there is indeed a problem, but much false information has worked its way into the popular imagination, while little of the actual empirical evidence has. The subject is fraught with erroneous reporting, feminist rhetoric, male apology, distorted facts, and, frankly, bogeymen.

Common sense dictates that football is not the culprit as much as the excessive celebration of it is. Steroid abuse, binge drinking, rape banter, the pressure by coaches to be tough, mixed messages of groupies, exalted status and an exaggerated sense of entitlement from years of being let off the hook, recruited by sorority hostesses, and tossed freebies—those are the things that cause sexually violent behavior. Not blocking and tackling.

Think about it. A group of physically gifted young men are hatched in a cross-culture of rape jokes and besotted excess and taught that Hamburger Helper comes with a real person. Actually, it's a wonder more of them aren't marauding monsters.

A few clear answers are available. Here is a basic handbook for women on associating with football players:

1) individually, they're fine. but in groups . . .

Athletes are more likely than average citizens to commit gang rape. They are joined in this regard by frat boys and soldiers. Anthropologist Peggy Sanday has found that men in sex-segregated groups, whether fraternities, sports teams, or the military, are more likely to engage in group sexual assault. Alcohol abuse, separate housing, emotional platoonlike cohesion (or bonding), and shower-room boasting of sexual conquests are well documented as being contributing factors. Sociologists, incidentally, don't classify rape as a form of sexuality but as a form of violence and view it less as a result of psychological factors than social ones. Meaning, it's not a result of your screwed-up childhood but of your screwed-up society.

Sanday has found that the frequency of rape varies greatly from one tribe or society to another and calls societies with the abovementioned segregated sex characteristics "rape cultures." Environments that eroticize notions of male domination, coupled with the tolerance of violence, are fertile petri dishes of aggressive behavior toward women. Sociologists have noted striking similarities between sports cultures and rape cultures.

Sorry, guys. You're busted.

2) it's probably okay to go on a date with a football player, but keep an eye on how much he drinks

What little empirical evidence exists on the subject of athletes and single or "simple" rape has caused rifts among social scientists, some of whom contend that football players have been unfairly tarred by misleading statistics. But they all agree that alcohol in combination with a gridiron mentality equals a menace.

In 1993, a social scientist at the University of Arizona, Mary Koss, conducted a study entitled

The Prediction of Sexual Aggression by Alcohol Use, Athletic Participation, and Fraternity Affiliation. Koss examined a single Division I college campus and found that nicotine and alcohol use were "strongly associated" with the incidence of sexual assault and that varsity athletic participation in a revenue-producing sport was "weakly" associated.

In 1994, a study jointly undertaken by a team from Northeastern University and the University of Massachussetts–Amherst found a seemingly significant connection between athletes and sexual assault. They examined reports of sexual assault to the judicial affairs offices of ten large universities from 1991 to 1993 and found that, while athletes represented just 3.3 percent of the overall male student population, they represented 19 percent of the reported incidences. Sixty-seven percent of the athletes played football or basketball.

Todd Crosset, an assistant professor of sports management at the University of Massachusetts–Amherst and a coauthor of the study, has profoundly mixed emotions about the attention the work has received since publication. "I'm in the midst of a moral panic," he says. Crosset was dismayed at the way the press seized on the study and particularly on the word "significant" used to describe their statistical findings.

In fact, the authors went to great lengths to

stress the limitations of their study. For one thing, there were 3 million crimes against women reported in 1995. For another, it's estimated that 84 percent of all rapes go unreported. In that context, athletes may be an extremely insignificant part of the overall sexual assault problem. "I feel, on the one hand, that the issue has been exaggerated," Crosset says. "It's way out of whack. When you look at violence against women and the overall numbers, athletes are a speck. For instance, at the University of Texas, athletes are 1 percent of the overall population. So you think, 'Geez, those guys would have to be awfully busy.' "

Part of the problem, Crosset says, is that "significant" means two different things to reporters and statisticians. "All it means is that something is going on," he says. "Now, what is it? Is it that they drink more? Maybe. What have we proved? Nothing yet. We're gathering evidence."

One researcher who takes exception to the conclusions in the study is Dr. Richard Lapchick of the Center for the Study of Sport in Society at Northeastern, where it was originally initiated. Lapchick found the work "fundamentally flawed" because there was no control for alcohol, tobacco, and attitudes toward women, which, again, are the three primary predictors for sexual aggression.

Lapchick says when Crosset's study is stated in

straight numbers rather than percentages, it loses some of its impact: In sixty-five cases reported at ten campuses over three years, thirteen of the accused were athletes and seven were football or basketball players. Lapchick does not consider the figures consequential. "There is no conclusive study at this point," Lapchick declares.

But Crosset, who was a swimmer at Texas and an athletic director at Dartmouth, cautions that NFL officials and NCAA athletic directors will use such a statement as a way of ducking the issue, something they are all too prone to do. The company line is that athletics are a microcosm of society and therefore nothing is their fault.

"The standard song and dance is 'Things are bad all over and we're no worse than anybody else,'" Crosset says. "To me, that's an abdication of responsibility. There is violence against women in every community, and in each one it's slightly different and that community is obliged to address it. Athletes are obliged to address the problem, the same way they ought to address the problem of concussions or knee injuries, and they don't have to wait for the egghead social scientists to do it."

3) it's okay to watch the super bowl with your husband

Men do not commit domestic abuse at a higher rate on Super Bowl Sunday. There is not a shred of empirical evidence to support such a thing. Nevertheless, the notion has been widely disseminated, published by newspapers from Philadelphia to San Francisco and by feminist author Mariah Burton Nelson. It is not only a specious theory, it is an irresponsible one, because it trivializes the frequency and cause of domestic violence. Women are beaten at a rate of every fifteen seconds. Not just on Sundays.

"That statistic's been apologized for, hopefully," Crosset says.

How did it get started? From anecdotal reports at women's shelters. However, anecdotal evidence is not scientific evidence. On closer examination, spousal abuse experts find that women's shelters experience a rise in calls to hotlines on all Sundays—not just autumn ones. That may be because the man of the house is home all day.

Similarly, court records indicate that women obtain more restraining orders in the summer, when the kids are out of school and it's easier to move them.

At the Houston Area Women's Center, volunteers were curious about the controversial claim, so they tracked hotline calls on Super Bowl Sunday over a five-year period. They found no marked increase. Moreover, tracking hotline calls was hardly a rigorous scientific method, because the numbers of calls fielded depended on how many volunteers were available to answer the

185

phones. "It's very, very iffy," said spokesperson Mitzi Vorachek.

According to Vorachek, anecdotal evidence of domestic abuse around football is once again much more likely to be related to drinking than to the game itself. Reports of domestic abuse jump significantly on holidays, when booze flows, everyone is in the house, company arrives, and arguments break out. Larry Wenner of *The Journal of Sport and Social Issues* says of the Super Bowl claim, "There are a variety of things going on there. Alcohol is involved, responsibilities aren't attended to, tensions rise. There are repercussions, no matter what the event. Those figures are all goofy. People talk about them, but when you ask for them, they have trouble getting them. They never materialize."

4) if you have a problem with a football player, don't expect any justice from coaches, owners, commissioners, university administrators, or league officials

The biggest problem in football is not violent men. It's their apologists. If there is a stereotype evolving, the wrongheaded values of the NCAA and NFL are responsible.

What on earth does it say about the NFL that former Houston Oilers tackle David Williams was fined by the team and faced suspension for refusing to travel to a game when his wife was in labor with their firstborn child in 1994, while sexual assault and domestic abuse go largely unpunished by teams?

When Williams stayed by his wife's hospital bed, offensive line coach Bob Young said furiously, "They ought to suspend him for a week, maybe two . . . That's, like, if World War II was going on and you said, 'I can't go fly. My wife is having a baby.' "

Yet when Minnesota Vikings quarterback Warren Moon, a Houston resident and onetime NFL Man of the Year, was booked on a misdemeanor assault charge for brawling with his wife, his agent, Leigh Steinberg, was outraged. "What societal value is protected by arresting Warren Moon?" he said indignantly.

Prosecutors refused to drop the case. Testimony revealed that the Moons were involved in three incidences of domestic violence in 1986. Moon was found innocent when his wife, Felicia, testified that she started the fight.

On November 13, 1994, *The Washington Post,* under the headline VIOLENCE IN FOOTBALL EXTENDS OFF THE FIELD, published a review of police files from 1989 to 1994 and found that 141 football players—56 pro and 85 college—were reported for violent behavior toward women. Of those 56 pros,

187

43 were on active NFL rosters at the time of the alleged incidents. There are 1,500 players in the NFL. Statistically, that would seem "significant."

And yet, at the time of the *Post* report, NFL commissioner Paul Tagliabue had sanctioned just one player during his tenure.

Violence against women is about power and entitlement and when league officials seem to ignore the issue, they exacerbate it, perpetuating the athlete's problem. Why shouldn't a guy think he can assault with impunity? Vance Johnson, the former star receiver for the Denver Broncos, admitted in his powerful autobiography that he committed domestic abuse. Johnson was one of eight Broncos accused of assaults against women in 1990–91. He cowrote his book with teammate Reggie Rivers, a rookie that year who was appalled by the behavior of his teammates. Together they tried to explain the causes.

"To me, it's less about the football field than it is about power issues," Rivers says. "Look. I've got seventy-six thousand people watching me every weekend. Women flock to me. I go to a restaurant and I get the best table, and everyone wants my autograph. The owner picks up the check. Then I go home and my wife treats me like just another guy. So I lash out to assert my power."

Crosset says that Rivers is on to something. "If they get their way all the time, their skills of negotiating normal adult relations atrophy," he says. "So they may be more likely to resort to a physical response."

That's why Nebraska coach Tom Osborne's decision to reinstate running back Lawrence Phillips after he attacked his girlfriend during the 1995 season was so unpardonable. When Osborne took Phillips back into the fold and allowed him to star in the national championship game in the Fiesta Bowl, citing Phillips's troubled childhood as an orphan, he played right into a batterer's skewed sense that *he* is the true victim. And into the male fantasy that if you are good enough, you can get away with anything.

Osborne spoke like another son of Nebraska, Father Flanagan, who once said, rather stupidly, "There are no bad boys." Guess what? There *are* bad boys. There are serious, serious badasses.

Had Osborne been smarter, he would have realized that in the post–O.J. climate, the game could not stand another attack on a woman without suffering a serious—and perhaps irretrievable—credibility problem.

If guys want to correct the stereotypes, then they should start correcting the real problem. No, violent behavior is not rampant in football. But it is condoned, if not subtly encouraged, to a degree not found in the rest of society. Even the military is better these days at voicing the proper sentiments than football authorities are. If an admiral tolerated Phillips's behavior, he'd be forcibly retired.

The next time a college player assaults his girlfriend he should be disciplined by his team, *and* his university, *and* the law. The next time a pro player rapes a girl or assaults his wife— or anybody else, for that matter—he should be disciplined by his team, *and* the league, *and* the law. It should be a standard clause in every contract.

And yet the NFL and NCAA consistently refuse to make such rules, claiming sexual violence is a societal ill and governed by the courts. Any NFL official will tell you that it's not "the business of the league."

The claim doesn't wash. Both of those august institutions have sanctions for drug use and gambling. Why? Could it be because *those* societal ills were beginning to hurt the marketability of the sport and fans were beginning to question its integrity?

The NFL and the NCAA had better wise up, because in their seeming tolerance of violence against women they have created a serious perception problem. Forty-three active players assaulting women. If that's not the business of the league, then what is? Licensing, apparently.

The O. J. Simpson trial was the Watergate of

football; it made female football fans forever cynical. We don't trust our Jack Armstrongs anymore. Underneath it all we're wondering, "Yeah, but what's the son of a bitch like when he gets home?"

the mouths *of* *babes* II

THE FOLLOWING is a transcript of the first nationally televised NFL Women's League football game, played between the expansion Washington First Ladies and the New Jersey Steinems. It was broadcast from Atlantic City on September 12, 2022.

The NFL expanded to include a women's division, becoming the NFL&WL, after the so-called Domestic Riots of 2021 resulted in the destruction by arson of several major stadiums around the country, including Candlestick Park, Three Rivers Stadium, and Veterans Stadium. Marauding groups of women set ablaze some of the nation's most historic and beloved home fields in protest of the NFL's refusal to comply with Title LXXX, the federal legislation requiring all pro leagues to provide equal access to female competitors. The league finally capitulated.

"Sorry, guys. The harpies held a gun to my head," NFL Commissioner Michael Cuomo said.

Calling the action for NBC–MicroApple Systems were Jay Montana, the grandson of former Super Bowl quarterback Joe Montana; Spike Ditka, the nephew of former Chicago Bears great Mike Ditka; and Cody Gifford, a man well known to you all.

Reporting from the sidelines was noted feminist author Caitlin Baggin Nozzle. Nozzle achieved some prominence in the early 2000s for her books theorizing that football was a "homoerotic manifestation" and "an agent of misogynistic expression" against women. She contended that football represented an exercise in which men use their bodies as missiles, thereby posing an inherent threat of sexual violence toward the opposite sex.

Nozzle's critics claimed she was permanently mad at football because when she was in college her women's lacrosse team didn't have enough money for new kneesocks, while the football players got a brand-new soft ice cream machine for their cafeteria.

NBC–MicroApple's decision to televise the contest between the Steinems and the First Ladies was extremely controversial and occurred only at the insistence of network owner Susan Saint

James, who inherited the company from her late husband, former General Electric majority stockholder Dick Ebersol.

gifford Welcome, everyone, to this historic occasion. Joining me are two gentlemen who, I think it's safe to say, are exactly as happy to be here as I am.

ditka Is it over yet?

gifford And here come the teams now. Boy, this crowd is going crazy. Listen to that shrieking.

ditka Estrogen poisoning.

gifford Let's go to our sideline reporter, Caitlin Baggin Nozzle. Caitlin, what's it like down there?

nozzle Well, Cody, it's a pretty exciting thing to be a woman tonight. Groups have come from everywhere. In the northeast corner of the end zone, ACT OUT has put up a giant banner.

gifford And the kick is up! Appleby returns it to the twenty-one for the First Ladies.

montana Those of you watching at home have probably noticed the field is shaped a little differently tonight. Don't worry, folks. That's just landscaping.

gifford Those things you see in the end zones are bright rows of tulips. Heh-heh.

montana What are those things along the team benches?

gifford Ficus trees.

ditka All I can say is, they better put everything back the way they found it.

gifford You know, Jay, I think teal *is* a good color for a uniform.

montana The Steinems are in taupe. Team owner Martina Navratilova said the color was chosen to reflect the hair color of their namesake, the late great Gloria Steinem.

gifford Bond rolls right, finds Breakstone for twelve! And there's a flag on the play. We should tell you that the rules are slightly different in the Women's League. For an explanation, let's go back to our sideline reporter, Caitlin Baggin Nozzle.

nozzle Thanks, Cody. First of all, there are no captains. The head coach of the First Ladies, Maude Yard, explained to me that they chose *not* to model their league after what she called "the antiquated male hierarchy." And may I just say that I heartily commend them for it.

gifford In fact, they don't even call themselves teams, do they?

nozzle That's right. They're "cooperatives."

ditka Jesus Christ.

nozzle Second, some of the terminology may be unfamiliar to you. That's because the names of

195

the penalties have also been changed. Interference is no longer interference. It's "inappropriate behavior." And encroachment is now "harassment."

gifford Bond is scrambling! She's in trouble! And she's sacked all the way back to the two! A safety has to be a concern.

nozzle Uh, Cody?

gifford Yes, Caitlin.

nozzle It's not a safety anymore, either.

montana What is it?

nozzle It's called "that stupid thing."

gifford Bond hands off to Shriner, gain of three.

nozzle That play is called Thelma and Louise and basically what Shriner does is explode up the middle.

gifford Bond to Breakstone, deep! Breakstone to the forty, the thirty, the ten! She scores! Spike, explain what happened on that play.

ditka I wasn't really paying attention, but it looked a little bit like football.

gifford The extra point is good. And that's the half. Let's go back down to Caitlin Baggin Nozzle, who is with Bond as she heads into the locker room.

nozzle Carry, tell us about that glorious touchdown.

bond The play is called Salute to Sally Ride. Pam was really chanting to herself in the huddle.

She has a little self-esteem poem she likes to recite. And I just said to her, "I totally support you in your effort."

(*Halftime Show.* Segment 1: A profile of Dottie Norville, quarterback for the Steinems, granddaughter of the late TV personality. Segment 2: Highlights from the child-care center in the basement of the stadium.)

gifford And we're back for the second half. The kick rolls through the end zone and the Steinems will take over.

montana You know, I couldn't help noticing that the food at the concessions has really undergone a sweeping change.

ditka Yeah. You can't get anything decent thing to eat.

gifford The old *Take Me Out to the Ball Game* fare has been replaced by some very elegant cuisine. Instead of hot dogs, we've got arugala salads and a variety of pastas, in halves or shares.

montana I had fennel soup and the spinach fettuccine, followed by a mochaccino.

gifford Here comes Norville, on a bootleg, for five!

ditka No beer. Everywhere you look, nothing but spritzers.

197

gifford Norville, play-action to Bonner, for twelve!

nozzle That play is called Three-Bean Veggie Casserole and it relies heavily on decoys.

gifford Bronfman off-tackle for four. Bronfman gets up a little slowly after that play. She really took a blow from the linebacker, Bailey.

ditka Sugar britches.

montana Look at those two glare at each other. I'd like to see them grease up and go at it on late-night cable.

nozzle But, you know, they're talking about it and they're going to resolve it.

gifford And there's the two-minute warning. We apologize to all of you at home for the length of time these teams are spending in the huddle. That's because there's no twenty-five-second clock. It's a five-minute clock.

montana Why is that?

nozzle So everyone gets to evaluate their feelings.

ditka Bunch of yakety boxes.

gifford Norville to Wilsey, deep! Wilsey at the twenty, the ten, and she scores!

nozzle Cody, that play is called Split-Level Colonnade with Elegant Crown Molding and Avocado Interior, and didn't it live up to its billing!

gifford And time expires! The final score is . . . ! Hey, what *is* the final score?

nozzle There isn't one.

ditka What do you mean, there isn't one?

nozzle They decided not to keep score.

ditka Why the hell not?

nozzle Because it's the *process* that's important.

(Ditka rips out his cables. The screen goes to black.)

why are those women trying to kill football?

DO WOMEN really want to compete with guys? For a lot of us nonideologues, the honest and emphatically unrhetorical answer is "Not really."

Why not?

Because we don't want to butt heads with a lot of guys, that's why not.

The feminine quest for total male sports acceptance will get knocked back on its ass every time by the fact that we do not have the upper-body muscle mass that guys do. Trying to play with guys at their favorite big-money sports is probably a futile, not to mention questionable, aspiration. The egghead social scientist term for the physical differences between men and women is the Muscle Gap.

The Muscle Gap is why, in the end, Dinosaur Guys really only have one use for us.

Two Dinosaur Guys are watching a women's tennis match.

why are women trying to kill football?

dino guy 1 Would you do her?
dino guy 2 I don't really know her, so, probably.

For years, Dinosaur Guys have used the Muscle Gap to suggest that women athletes are charity cases. They insinuate that because women don't play varsity and pro football, we are second-class athletic citizens. Of course, women shouldn't have to take a hit to prove we are entitled to compete at the sport of our choice. That's what Congress is for. Title IX legislation states that universities receiving federal funds must devote similar funding to women's sports that they do to men's. But even though Title IX has been federal law since 1972, *90 percent of the schools in this country do not comply with it*, according to the Women's Sports Foundation. These schools claim they cannot spare any loose change from football, despite the fact that men's sports annually receive $179 million more scholarship monies.

The fact of the female build is extremely problematic. Women must constantly cast about for ways to prove our athletic worth in a society in which football is considered the competitive standard. Our basic dilemma—the guilty thought that lurks in the back of our minds—is that maybe guys are right. Maybe the games women play really are less important than football.

So what do we do?

We make fun of it.

That's why women are so sarcastic on the subject of the gridiron. We are like smaller players trying to outwit bigger players. If we can somehow cut the legs out from under guys, gender equity in sports might be easier to achieve.

Mary Jo Kane of the University of Minnesota's Center for Research on Girls and Women in Sport specializes in the kind of judo-flip argument that babes are best at. Kane says we should develop new athletic standards that emphasize things other than strength. She says female athletic accomplishment should be viewed on a "continuum" rather than subverted into a rigid win-lose framework. For instance, when a top female marathoner is compared to the first-place men's time, we stress the fact that she places sixtieth overall, behind fifty-nine men. We overlook the fact that she dusted thirty-five hundred other elite male runners.

Using the same reasoning, here are some other frequently overlooked ways in which females routinely outstrip male performance: We have withstood 80 million more labor contractions, put up with 400 million more patronizing remarks, and washed, laundered, rinsed, dried, and stacked 100 million more objects than guys have, from shirts to plates.

"Many women routinely outperform men in

physical activity, and I'm not talking ballet," Kane says. "But what you walk away with is 'No matter how good she is, she can never beat men.' Instead, we should be saying, 'She can beat almost all of the men out there.'"

Kane is subverting right back. Resubversiveness. It is a wonderful technique and something women should do more of, instead of screaming.

The Modern Woman's best friend, Missy, is a terrific resubversive. Consider the way she dealt with her daughter, Molly, the last time they went to a toy store.

"I want Beach Barbie," Molly said.

"She's dead," Missy said. "She drowned. Her inner tube didn't inflate."

The only flaw in Kane's argument is: You can't redefine traditional sports values overnight. Most people—and not just men—prefer big-time team sports that involve propelling a ball through space and other muscle-mass activities. Also, they like to celebrate absolute winners, not someone who finished sixtieth.

Millions of babes didn't watch the Super Bowl because they were oppressed by male social constructions of the concept of victory.

So what's the answer? Maybe we should simply have different standards for men and women. Call it a day and sit at separate tables. It's one possibility, although a controversial one. Such a solution is called sex segregation and it has a number of supporters, but an equal number of detractors.

There is intriguing evidence that girls benefit from sex-segregated classrooms, instead of coed ones where their confidence gets stifled by fledgling Boy Pigs who hog all the teachers' time by being so restive and shouting the answers out of turn. Ever notice how Attention Deficiency Disorder is strictly a guy thing? Sex segregation is just like getting two TVs, his and hers, so he'll stop driving us crazy with the remote control, which he wields like an electronic penis substitute.

Some feminists would call this "ghettoizing" or "marginalizing" women's sports and say that it can be used as an excuse to perpetuate inequalities. But, again, the question we have to ask ourselves is: Do we really want acceptance from the Guy Mainstream and are we ever likely to get it? Because if we do, it's going to mean watching an awful lot of Steven Seagal movies on cable.

Why is it that saying women are *different* is so often interpreted as saying we are inferior, even by other feminists?

The truth is that the various factions in the women's sports movement don't really agree on what they want, and this makes the going even slower. Perfect Equality? Separate Equality? Virtual Equality? Mostly, it seems like what we want is Sort of Equality But Strictly on Our Own Terms. Sports like football are especially fraught with danger for women, because we get tangled up in our politics. If we say it's okay to hold women to separate standards, then what happens to the proposition of equal work for equal pay?

It's all very tricky.

There is only one real solution.

Women need to be Bigger Pigs.

We have still greater Pig Potential that we must tap into more fully.

Guys don't worry about philosophical questions like gender equity. Why? Because they're pigs. They just assume they have an inalienable right to play football, whether they're any good at it or not. Every weekend they claim the playgrounds and the public parks of this country like a bunch of glorified Spartacuses.

There are many things women can do to improve their lot in sports without the help of Congress.

1) We must start by refusing to fall into political-ethical quandaries. Women should assume an inalienable right to play and take the field in the same high-handed gladiatorial style that guys do. Who cares if we're any good or not? The lowliest men's Division III team assumes a big-man-

on-campus status wholly unearned, so why shouldn't we?

2) We should build Private Parks for Women, devoted to female recreational leagues. If the guys want to play on our fields, make them sue us for a change. Or better yet, rent them from us.

3) We need to start throwing our money around. Women don't know how to write really big checks yet. The reason football is such a rich sport is because rich guys throw money at it. Benefactors build parks and stadiums and name them after themselves. Wealthy alumni drown college programs in endowents. Corporate execs buy sky boxes.

Where are all the rich women? They should be spending their dough on struggling women's clubs, instead of Escada.

4) Title IX doesn't go nearly far enough. What we need is some radical change. Here is what we should be lobbying Congress to force the NCAA to do.

A) Reduce all college football teams to thirty-three players and make the offense and defense play both ways.

B) Make freshmen ineligible.

C) Eliminate much of the needless gear, thereby reducing costs.

D) Do away with spring practices.

They can keep bowl games, big stadiums, and All-American teams.

Guys would scream, of course. What would their precious game look like?

It would look like 1938.

That's how the game used to be played.

The benefits of athletic participation for women are incontrovertible: Unwanted pregnancy and osteoporosis decrease, graduation rates soar, and so does the female rate of success in business.

Girls are frequently stronger than boys in preadolescence and have no problem competing with them at a variety of sports. But female sports participation numbers drop sharply when they reach high school. The main reason is that opportunities for girls tail off for lack of funding and for lack of encouragement.

Forget guys. The athletic success of women hasn't been a priority among other *women*. And we expect guys to help us? They aren't going to, at least not voluntarily. So we might as well stop being so afraid of What Guys Might Say and preoccupied with How We Compare to Them. We need to Stop Looking in the Mirror. It's always going to look like a funhouse reflection as long as we stand next to NFL players, who come from the absolute extreme end of the male physical spectrum.

Subverse away. Remember. Right now, there are twenty yahoos at your local public park—paunchy, dorky, middle-aged guys—playing touch football with the backing of their local hardware outlet and thinking of themselves as Joe Montanas. All that should matter to babes is getting in the game.

A prizewinning subversive is Donna Lopiano. Lopiano is a fabulous pig. She has a theory that women are actually better-suited to play football. Women, she claims, carry their reproductive organs *inside* their bodies. "The ovaries have a natural protective housing," she says. "Men, who carry their organs on the outside, are the ones we should really be worrying about."

The position Lopiano really aspires to in life is a monarchy, because then she could tell everybody what to do. As there are no vacant thrones, she will settle for the role of That Woman Who's Trying to Kill Football, as she is known among her enemies. Her actual title is executive director of the Women's Sports Foundation and in that capacity Lopiano contends she doesn't really want to kill football, she just wants to curb its wretched excess. But try telling that to whiny control-freak coaches and administrators who are afraid of losing their comfortable way of life.

It's a sign of some success that Lopiano is referred to in the plural by her adversaries. "The Lopianos," College Football Association executive director Chuck Neinas calls her, as in "The Lopianos of the world are the ones who have coined the phrase 'gender equity' and turned this into a 100-yard battlefield." It's a backhand compliment, since there's only one of her.

Lopiano has developed an off-with-their-heads manner from years of dealing with recalcitrant stonewalling by coaches and administrators on the issue of Title IX. Ever since the law was written, schools have been trying to weasel around it—with varying degrees of success. The problem with the statute is that if NCAA schools truly complied with its letter and spirit, they might have to downsize the sacred cow, football, which, while it can be the big moneymaker, is more often the costliest of all sports. No one is willing to knock a couple of hooves off. Except for Lopiano.

Every day Lopiano dresses up in what she refers to as her combat gear—her makeup is her "war paint, like eye black," her high heels are her "power shoes"—and does battle in the war of the sexes. Lopiano's agenda is simple and, according to some diehard football fans, deeply un-American: If Title IX can't be enforced without taking a bite out of some of the most popular big-time teams in the country, then so be it.

Texas men's athletic director DeLoss Dodds once said, after Lopiano almost got hit by falling brick, "If anything hits her head, her head'll break it." But it would be easier to dismiss Lopiano if she hadn't spent over fifteen years as women's athletic director at Texas, where she built a model of moneymaking excellence and amassed boxcars of evidence, both statistical and anecdotal, to support her claims that football is a chief agent of sexism at the collegiate level.

That national championships are not necessarily won with excess was proven by Lopiano's Longhorn teams, which won seventeen NCAA championships over ten years on a shoestring budget. It is interesting to note that the Texas women's athletic department was sex-segregated: It had its own staff. When Lopiano arrived at Texas in 1975, she found little more than a ladies' auxiliary collection of hit-and-giggle clubs. The women's basketball team still wore kilts. She dreamed up crazy marketing schemes to raise money and attendance. She took a cannonball leap from a high-dive tower and kissed Bevo the Longhorn on the nose at a halftime ceremony. When Lopiano left, the Texas women's program had an annual bottom line of $3.7 million. (This was still dwarfed by the $12 million men's budget.)

Lopiano's opponents like Neinas contend that football supports all other non-revenue-producing sports and to weaken it by cost cutting or to punish it by reducing scholarships doesn't make sense. "Why deprive kids of an opportunity to play?" he says. The problem is that Neinas doesn't mean kids, he means *boys*. According to

Lopiano: 1) at about 80 percent of all NCAA institutions, football doesn't even pay for itself, much less for women's sports; 2) sixty-two percent of all major football programs ran annual deficits of over a half million dollars as of 1993; and 3) women got only 33 percent of all scholarship money in 1995.

In short, football doesn't make money for schools, as opponents of Title IX claim. It spends it hand over fist. Lopiano once remarked that she would have to buy her women's basketball team chinchilla warmups to equal the free-spending ways of the men's programs.

Lopiano's talent for stating the obvious has been especially useful in the Title IX discussions before Congress, as the College Football Association has appealed for special relief from the law. Her point is: If the Texas women's teams could win all those NCAA titles on next to no money, how come guys scream that football can't stand a trim without *dying?*

Guys have a very low pain threshold. A guy nicks himself with a hedge clipper and he acts like he needs a prosthesis.

Why, Lopiano wants to know, do NCAA Division I teams insist on staying in hotels the night before *home* games, running up huge bills?

Why do football teams require full juice bars in their locker rooms, instead of a simple refrigera-

211

tor? Why do schools need glossy four-color brochures and 120-page media guides that cost more than the annual reports of some major corporations?

Why did a major university spend $120,000 changing the wood paneling in the office of the head coach from oak to mahogany?

Lopiano felt a certain gleeful satisfaction when she was accosted once by Neinas during an NCAA convention. Neinas stormed across a room, red-faced, and said, "Lopiano, we're *staying* in hotels!"

"Football," Lopiano says, "is afraid of losing its standard of living."

Another chief motivation behind male administrators' resistance to Title IX, of course, is that Dinosaur Guys are afraid of the Scary New Women who might arise from it.

As well they should be.

Dino Guys are disconcerted by the idea of all these combative girls playing sports. They are especially disconcerted by the idea of them playing contact sports, even against each other. If it turns out women can take a hit, then that's one more of life's certainties tragically eroded.

"Why do we fear women hitting other women?" asks egghead social scientist Todd Crosset. "Because then men wouldn't know how to define themselves."

why are women trying to kill football?

Dino Guys, meet the Henderson girls.

The Henderson girls are terrifying examples of Scary New Women. They are what can happen when you give girls equal opportunity. They represent that first generation of young women who have played contact sports from the time they were small girls and who have played them side by side with their brothers and dates—with the wholehearted approval of their fathers.

Check out how a Modern Father reacts when someone tries to tell him that his daughter isn't allowed to play. He takes it personally.

In 1988, when Jessica Henderson was twelve, she decided to try out for her local Pop Warner team in Oakton, Virginia. But when she showed up, league officials told her that she couldn't play.

Jessica is the daughter of Harold Henderson, the NFL's general counsel and executive vice president, and she is nobody's fool, least of all yours. She went home and told Daddy.

"I had to have some conversations with them," Harold says casually.

Suffice it to say Jessica got her tryout. Then practice started. Since the coaches couldn't run her off legally, they tried to run her off literally. They put all the toughest drills at the start of the first practice, hoping she'd quit. "She was the smallest one out there and she took a beating," Harold says.

There were two rules in the Henderson household. You never, ever quit anything. And you had to be good at everything. Jessica and her sister, Kim, played five sports and two musical instruments, piano and flute. Their mother, Franzine, a teacher, spent every afternoon in the car from 3 P.M. to 8 P.M., shuttling kids to lessons and practices: soccer practices, swimming practices, volleyball practices, basketball practices. They even ran 10 k's.

The day of the season opener came. The first time Jessica touched the ball, she scored on a sixty-five-yard punt return.

So they made her the starting tailback and safety.

Then Jessica led the team in rushing touchdowns and tackles.

So they made her captain.

People from all over the neighborhood came to see Jessica lead a team that finished second in their region. This is how good she was: She completely overshadowed her brother, Harold III, who was also a running back on the team. And Harold was no slouch. He would eventually become a 1,000-yard rusher for Oakton High.

Jessica came close to getting hurt just once, in a head-on collision with an opposing player on a punt return. Everybody gasped. But she just jumped right up. "The other kid spent the rest of

214

the game on the bench with his mother," Kim Henderson says.

After two years, Jessica quit and went back to her first love, soccer. The reason was that she had no future in football. She wasn't ever going to be big enough to play at the position she wanted, wide receiver, and she refused to be a stupid kicker. So Harold III became the local high school star, and Jessica eventually got a soccer scholarship to Harvard.

When Jessica hung up her cleats, the Hendersons breathed a sigh of relief. They thought their days of worrying about permanent injury were over. Then Kim, a freshman up at Princeton, called home.

"I made the rugby team," she said. "I think we can win a national championship."

"Is that the crazy sport where they don't wear pads and tackle each other?" Franzine said.

Kim said it was. There was a pause on the other end of the line. Then Franzine said something no one in the family ever thought they would hear her say.

"You can quit any time you want," she said.

From then on, the Hendersons called Princeton on a weekly basis to make sure their oldest daughter was still alive. The first time they went to a game, they thought they might not recover. Rugby made football look genteel. Rugby was about mud

215

and bare-knuckled brawling, with a keg of beer and meat chops afterward. Rugby was *worse* than football.

"All I could think was 'There goes all that orthodontist work,' " Harold Sr. says. "I just knew she was bound to be permanently disfigured."

Princeton was a hotbed of Dinosaur Guys. Actually, sexism was one of Kim's chief motivations in playing rugby. She wanted revenge. Princeton did not admit women until 1973—and even then, it admitted only one. There was a lingering assumption that the coed women weren't as intellectually competitive as the men. "I'd sit there in the seminars and feel like killing someone," Kim says. So she took it out on the field. She loved piling into a scrum, burying her shoulders into the body of an opponent.

The 1995 Princeton women's rugby national championship squad was a remarkable collection of women from disparate backgrounds. There were sorority girls, socialites, premeds, art history majors. Michael Eisner's niece was a member. Then there was Yusi Wang, who played viola in the school orchestra and drove a motorcycle to practice. Kim, a 125-pound scrum half, worked in a florist shop part-time. Alexandra Bernbach came from a Park Avenue family. Christine Leporati was five-foot-two, 110 pounds of soft-spokenness, and the fastest, toughest girl on the team. "She tackled anything that moved," Kim says.

Since rugby wasn't a varsity sport, they got only $1,800 a year in funding from the school administration. The rest of their $18,000 in expenses they had to raise themselves, with club dues, fundraisers, alumni donations, and T-shirt sales. They didn't care. They were on a four-year plan to win a championship.

During stretching sessions, they would talk about dates and earrings. Then the game would start and they would interlock arms for a scrum and get shiners, split lips, fractured wrists and ankles, concussions.

Sometimes at night they would go to formals with bruises on their faces. Taura Null of Dallas attended Casino Night, the most elegant, Gatsby-esque evening of the year, in black satin and a black eye.

"There was no better feeling than getting your guts stomped out—and coming back again," Kim says. "It was nice to be able to control when you were giving and when you were getting. You'd be in the mud, tackling, and four hours later in an evening gown with your hair upswept. And you'd think, 'Man, I can do anything.'"

They were coached by Alex Curtis, a Ph.D. student who had a falling out with the men's team and offered his services to the women's club. Curtis said he actually liked coaching them better because they didn't act like they knew everything. The only problem was, their chins would tremble when he benched somebody. They cried and they named their favorite plays after ice cream parlors and sandwich shops. They gained a reputation on-campus for eccentric behavior. People all over the campus made fun of them for rolling around in the mud. Actually, the women were behaving just like men who bond into a team. They would celebrate big victories with keg parties and run naked laps around the eating clubs, the social centers of the campus.

When they made it to the Final Four, rugby fever suddenly swept the campus. The Final Four was not for cute little girls' clubs. It was for national powers with scholarship programs. Nevertheless, the Tigers upset defending champion Air Force, 29–5, to set up a national title game against Penn State on their home field.

A huge throng turned out at Princeton on May 7, 1995. On the sidelines, Harold Sr. stared, astounded, at upper-crust mothers in fur coats, holding Coach bags and yapping little dogs, while they screamed in Eastern lockjaw accents, "Kill her, kill her!"

Among them was the mother of Alexandra Bernbach, who struggled to maintain her composure when Alexandra blocked a kick with her face and then took an elbow to her eye. "I thought she was going to have a fit," Harold says. Alexandra would still have the mickey and bruises on Graduation Day.

Kim scored three touchdowns to lead the Tigers to a 20–0 victory. They were the only Princeton team to bring home a national championship trophy that year.

When Kim was named an All-American and the tournament's most valuable player in the postgame trophy ceremony, Harold swept her up in a hug, with tears in his eyes. "I thought, 'I've finally made my dad proud of me,' " she said.

They stayed on the field for an hour afterward, celebrating. Then they had a swanky fund-raiser for the team and raised about $5,000. Afterward they did the nude Olympic dash around the eating clubs again.

Inside the Cap and Gown, students heard the shrieking.

"What's that?" someone said.

"It's just the women's rugby team" was the reply. "They're outside, naked again."

On the Saturday before graduation, the president of Princeton marched at the head of the annual Reunion Parade, wearing a women's rugby jersey and carrying a rugby ball. The class of 1973 asked the rugby women to please carry their banner. So they did. It seemed only fitting, especially since a lot of the women on the team had been born in 1973.

"Sometimes we took a lot of crap for not being feminine," Kim said months later, sitting in a Manhattan coffee shop. "But my team, we loved everything we went through. For most women, sharing means giving. Historically, we haven't been allowed to take. But this was giving and taking. If anything, it made us feel more feminine. We'd think, 'Oh, man, tomorrow our nails are going to be ruined, and we're going to look terrible.' But then the whistle would blow, and all we had in us was 'Win, win, win.' So I guess it depends on what you mean by femininity. Does it mean sitting in a sewing circle with our legs crossed? No, we didn't do that. To us, it meant doing whatever you want and still feeling feminine. It was femininity to the nth degree. It was control of the entire situation."

Who knows? Someday a babe may come along with the upper-body mass for football. As the Hendersons demonstrated to Oakton, Virginia, and Princeton, New Jersey, a single remarkable personality can account for more progress than a whole social movement. One Jackie Joyner-Kersee can reinvent womanhood simply by existing.

But whoever the Scary New Woman is, she doesn't *have* to play football or anything else against men to achieve full status. There is no such thing as a "proper" direction of the female sports evolution. It is not something that can be hammered out in the sports pages, in Congress, or in sociology journals. Maybe some babes want to be beer-guzzling, snack-snorting louts with baseball caps on backward, and some want to be earthy granola-girls with underarm hair, and some want to be buffed-body babe narcissists. All we require, thank you very much, is freedom of choice, and we will figure the rest out by ourselves.

In the meantime, we have only one use for Dinosaur Guys.

They look okay in tuxedos.

recipes

pigs in a blanket

BUY 5 (five) cans of Pillsbury dinner rolls or biscuits and 3 (three) packages of Oscar Mayer Little Smokies.

WHACK the cans against the kitchen counter so they explode with gratifying gunshot-like effect.

RIP open packages of sausages.

UNROLL biscuit or dinner roll dough.

SLASH into triangles.

DROP a Little Smoky into a dough triangle, making whistling sound like a B-52 over Berlin.

ROLL the dough up with sausage in it, leaving thumbprints.

SCOOP onto cookie sheet.

BAKE (optional) at 350 until golden brown.

PLACE red-hot cookie sheet on coffee table.

heart attack dip

16 (sixteen) ounces or 2 (two) BIG HUNKS of
cream cheese
1 (one) WHOLE JAR EACH OF:
  Mayo
  Bac*Os
  Bottled parmesan cheese
1 (one) lemon
2 (two) packages of instant onion soup mix
1 (one) box of frozen spinach
4 (four) boxes Premium saltine crackers

DUMP contents of boxes, bottles, jars, and
packages into large MIXING BOWL, except for
lemon and crackers.

SLICE and CRUSH lemon into bowl, seeds and
all.

GRIND and MASH ingredients together with
large spoon until semismooth.

SERVE with saltines or chips of choice.

testosterone treats for twenty

TAKE 1 (one) perfectly contented, unassuming, happy to be grazing in the lush fields, shot up beyond description with growth hormones and antibiotics, fuzzy warm brown and white COW.

SLAUGHTER it.

CALL PETE at the Butcher Block and have it cut into twenty steaks.

TURN ON the VCR and remove shoes—if they were ever on.

LIGHT THE GRILL and insert Dallas–Pittsburgh in the VCR.

BOIL 20 (twenty) baked potatoes.

FIND a DUDETTE to make a salad.

MAKE sexist comments to enhance overall experience.

BAKE 40 (forty) ears of appropriately formed phallic rods of CORN ON THE COB, the symbols of fertility and the inexorable brute forces of nature.

TURN UP the VCR.

ROUND UP all of your COOL DUDE AMIGOS and invite them over, but wait until twenty minutes before the food is ready. Preface each invitation with "Yo."

PLACE 2 (two) gallons WHOLE MILK on the table. No glasses.

SET OUT plastic knives and forks. Do not distribute.

PUT assorted MOSTLY EMPTY bottles of salad dressing on the table.

IGNORE finger indentations in butter and put in butter dish.

EAT.

ROUND OUT meal with JOVIAL discussions of the lost art of good old-fashioned open-field tackling.